D1286907

THE
LITTLE
BOOK
OF
SHOW
JUMPING

ANNE HOLLAND

The
History
Press
Ireland

First published 2015

The History Press Ireland
50 City Quay
Dublin 2
Ireland
www.thehistorypress.ie

British Library Cataloguing in Publication Data.
A catalogue record for this book is available from the British Library.

ISBN 978 1 84588 884 8

Typesetting and origination by The History Press

Printed in the UK by TJ International Ltd, Padstow, Cornwall

CONTENTS

ACKNOWLEDGEMENTS

Alison of www.bentvillhistory.blogspot.ie
All England Jumping Course, Hickstead
British Showjumping (Gemma Southall)
Daily Mail online
Daily Telegraph
Marijn Dubbeldam
Robert Fagan, Mullingar Equestrian Centre
Horse and Hound
Independent on Sunday
Grace Logan, Hickstead
Brendan McArdle
Peter McCartan
Genevieve Murphy
Mavis Murray
RDS (Royal Dublin Society), www.rds.ie
RTÉ Sport, www.rte.ie
Emma Southall
Alan Smith
The Irish Field (Leo Powell)
The Irish Times
Wales and West Showground, Chepstow, www.theshowground.com
Grania Willis
www.canterbanter.co.uk
www.hay-net.co.uk
www.horseandhound.co.uk
www.horsefix.com
www.horsesportireland.ie
www.irishhorsegateway.ie
www.ronaldduncanfoundation.co.uk
www.sickipedia.org

INTRODUCTION

As a child my show-jumping heroes and heroines were Alan Oliver on Red Admiral and Pat Smythe on Tosca, Prince Hal and Flanagan, along with Irishmen Seamus Hayes on Goodbye and Tommy Wade on Dundrum. The pony Stroller was my favourite of all time for his amazing feats against horses, of which more later.

My own brief show-jumping attempts were certainly memorable, if not exactly successful. It all began with my first pony when I was 13. Shindy was a little devil who used to put his tongue over the bit and bolt; he also had a buck that could have graced any rodeo show. We took part in a show-jumping class at a local gymkhana, cantered in and popped the first fence fine. Trouble was, the exit was then dead ahead of him and, as I tried to steer him towards the second jump, it was out of the exit he bolted. Of course, we weren't allowed to try again.

A decade later, with my point-to-point career under way, I was invited to take part in a jockeys' show-jumping class at a local show. I was both lent a horse and given some tuition in the fine art of show jumping by Cherrie Hatton-Hall of the renowned Moat House riding academy, Benenden, Kent. She was one of the country's top tutors, and numbered Princess Anne among her pupils.

The prize for the competition was to be a weekend in Paris for two; I can't remember the exact rules but I do know the fences gained extra points according to their rating. I was advised to keep circling round and round popping the one King fence. This seemed to be working and we were apparently well in the lead for that lovely prize when: crash! Down we came among a pile of poles. The horse, thank goodness, was fine, but I had broken my collar bone …

Fast forward another couple of decades to the horse of my life, a shining palomino part-bred Arab called Sunny. Together we contested a few Arab races and the remainder of his career was spent happily team-chasing and hunting. On one occasion the team chase also held a fun show-jumping class. We started off fine, but gradually Sunny gained speed and momentum so that finally, unable to make the tight turn to the final fence, we simply jumped the ropes out of the ring, doubtless scattering a few spectators in the process. A commentator at one team chase in Warwickshire likened him to David Broome's great Sunsalve with his style of jumping and added, 'I'd give my eye teeth for a day's hunting on this palomino.'

I gained a much closer insight into the sport when, for a number of years, I was *Horse and Hound* correspondent for junior show jumping, covering from the Midlands south. This job took me all over the southern half of England and Wales, where I watched and noted the stars of the future on their incredible JA ponies. It was a weekly column that I thoroughly enjoyed writing.

Sisters Michelle and Annette Lewis were two of 'my' riders. Pony-mad, from the East End of London, Annette developed a kick-back style with her legs (as had both Alan Oliver and Ted Edgar in earlier years), a habit she puts to having been so tall on her 12.2hh ponies that she was in danger of knocking poles with her own feet unless she threw them back and up. She became a successful adult rider and competed a number of times for England, but she may be best remembered for a dramatic attempt at the 10ft 6in bank in the Hickstead Derby. Horses are supposed to slide down the upper part, but in 1985 her grey horse Tutein jumped straight off the top. Inevitably they landed in a heap, but luckily both were uninjured and Tutein galloped off loose.

Another of 'my' juniors was Michael Mac, who tucked his growing frame neatly on his ponies; he became a successful adult rider and was chairman of the British Showjumping Association (BSJA) for five years from 2005 to 2013 (jointly that year with Les Harris), but sadly he died in 2014 aged just 52.

Show jumping endures as one of the most colourful, glamorous and exciting spectator sports of all, with those watching able to be much closer to the action than in many other sports. The men and women who take part are among the most skilful of athletes, and their magnificent, noble and courageous horses ensure admiration from all, and always will.

1

IN THE BEGINNING

THE 'LEAPING CONTEST'

The Lawn, Leinster House, Dublin 1868. Queen Victoria has been on the throne for 31 years, in what will prove to be slightly under half her reign. The Earl of Kildare, later the Duke of Leinster, built the fine Georgian house overlooking Merrion Square, in the heart of Georgian Dublin, but at this time it is headquarters of the Royal Dublin Society. In 1922 it will become home to the Dáil Éireann and Seanad Éireann, the two houses of the Oireachtas, the equivalent of the British Houses of Parliament. A handsome semi-circular double flight of steps at the Garden Front give access to Leinster Lawn.

Now, on this day, 30 July, in 1868, people are pouring through the gates and thronging round the lawn. In the centre is a high stone wall. Nothing else, apart from a number of horses being led around in hand at one end for various show classes; the rest is grass.

So why is the wall there? Reputedly standing 6ft high and topped with loose stones, it stands in isolated grandeur because today is the culmination of the three-day Leaping Contest, and the spectators want to see who will win the £10 prize and cup for this new spectacle.

Just one separate fence was jumped on the first two days, and only those who cleared the first day's fence could jump the next day, and if they cleared that also, they could progress to the final with the high wall. The original rules for leaping competitions were simply that the obstacles 'had to be cleared to the satisfaction of the judges'.

The prizes for the initial high and wide leaps were £5 for first and £2 for second, with £10 and a cup to the winner of the championship and £5 and a riding crop to the runner-up. The crowds flocked in, some 6,000 people in all.

The fence on day one was described as the high leap and was of timber, 4ft 6in high, trimmed with gorse. Day two was the wide leap: 12ft of water faced by gorse-filled timber. Day three was the stone wall, comprised of loose stones rising to a narrower top. Nine finalists had come through from the previous two days. The crowd watched with bated breath as Richard Flynn and his horse Shaun Rue beat off their eight rivals.

Flynn, a Strokestown, County Roscommon sheep farmer then sold Shaun Rue to Tom Conolly of Castletown, County Kildare for the enormous sum of £1,000 (roughly equivalent to £½ million today), who used him for hunting. Just two years short of a century later, in 1966, Tom's great-granddaughter, Diana Conolly-Carew, won the main RDS show-jumping event, the International Grand Prix, with Barrymore, so Castletown was once more home to Ireland's champion show jumper.

THE NATIONAL HORSE SHOW

While the 'leaping' was a novelty, there were also various in-hand (as opposed to ridden) classes which attracted 366 entries for a total prize fund of £520, and included classes for asses and mules. By 1870 the show was named 'The National Horse Show', and moved to August, the month in which it is still held; at that time it was combined with the Society's Annual Sheep Show.

Thomas Prior and Samuel Madden, themselves already members of the Dublin Philosophical Society, founded the Royal Dublin Society in 1731 in order to 'improve Husbandry, Manufactures and other Useful Arts'; a couple of weeks later the words 'and Sciences' were added. In other words, its aim was to promote the development of agriculture, industry, the arts and science. The word 'Royal' was added to its title when George IV became patron in 1820, five years after the purchase of Leinster House, and established a natural history museum there.

In 1879 the RDS acquired its present home in Ballsbridge, which was then open countryside and is now part of the fashionable 'D4' area of Dublin, and staged its horse show there for the first time in 1881 on 15 acres. In that year a viewing stand, capable of holding 800 people, was erected on the site of the present Grand Stand. By 1895 the leaping or jumping classes had become so popular that, with over 800 entries, it was necessary to run the jumping competitors off in pairs – causing considerable difficulties for the judges.

Since then the RDS has increased its prime-city site to 40 acres. Whichever part of the venue show-jumping fans visit, they will find current or future stars of the sport, now a world-wide phenomenon after those early days on the lawn in front of Leinster House, Dublin.

DID YOU KNOW?

Originally high jump (Puissance) competitions consisted of one single pole set at a height of 5ft (1.52m) but this style of competition had to be abandoned due to horses trying the easier option of going under the pole, risking the riders' heads, so more poles were added.

One of the first International Horse Shows at Olympia in 1907 boasted a schedule that read 'Jumping Competitions – over the whole course – open to the World.'

EARLY BRITISH SHOW JUMPING

The many Enclosure Acts, principally passed throughout the nineteenth century, led to the rise of horses jumping, in particular when young bloods out hunting pitted their horses and themselves against each other by leaping the newly grown hedges that now crisscrossed the land, especially in counties like Leicestershire. This was to have a knock-on effect on the embryonic sport of show jumping.

The hunting style of riding was with long stirrups and with riders sitting upright or leaning backwards over fences; after all, they would not know what was on the landing side: a ditch, a big drop, even a gate lying on the ground, perhaps, and they were less likely to fall off if already leaning backwards; this inevitably meant pulling the reins against the horse's mouth, impeding its natural flow and metaphorically pulling its back teeth out. It was also considered that it was better for the horse to take the weight on its hindquarters, and a notion took hold that the horse should be forced to land on its hind legs over a fence; this resulted in great discomfort for the horse, but it was the perceived wisdom of the day.

In show jumping the rider knows both the fences and the terrain in advance; what's more, the arena is generally fairly flat, but the same 'hunting' style was adopted throughout Europe.

Enter an Italian cavalry officer and instructor, one Federico Caprilli, for it was he who introduced the forward seat that soon became permanently adopted in show jumping. He believed, correctly, that this style would not impede the horse's balance while jumping, with the rider's weight being largely over the horse's shoulders, and his arms and hands sliding up the horse's neck, leaving the mouth free.

However, he was ridiculed (as was American jockey Tod Sloan when he brought the now-universal 'monkey on a stick' style to British horse racing at the end of the nineteenth century). Caprilli had watched and photographed horses jumping when loose and observed that on every occasion they landed on their front legs. Nevertheless, he was banished to a small cavalry school in southern Italy because of his beliefs; there he continued his experimentations with great success in equestrian competitions. As a result, the General Inspector of the Cavalry, HRH the Count of Turin, and the Commander of the Cavalry School of Pinerolo (near Turin) soon realised the genius and the value of Caprilli's methods and brought him as chief instructor to the Cavalry School of Pinerolo as well as its subsidiary in Tor di Quinto (near Rome).

Caprilli earned his reward by demonstrating his style in Greece in 1906 to an international audience at an early Olympic-type event. The Italian, French and Austrian cavalry schools, who had used the backward style, all adopted the Caprilli forward seat, and the rest of the world followed. Just one year later, at not yet 40, Caprilli lost consciousness while riding, fell and hit his head, and died.

It was in that same year, 1907, that London held its first international show, including show-jumping competitions, at Olympia. Two years later, at Olympia, Britain staged its first Nations Cup.

British Showjumping (www.britishshowjumping.co.uk, the official website of British Showjumping) describes the early judging methods:

Most participants were of a military background, with inter-country competitions for a team trophy, this later developed with sufficient civilian show jumpers for some of the competitions to be divided into Military and Civilian sections.

The judging decisions were arbitrary – some marked according to severity of obstacle, others on style. Prior to 1907 no marks were deducted for refusals though a competitor may have been asked to continue to the next obstacle for the sake of the spectators. Competitions could continue for as many rounds as the judges saw fit and often those with the least knockdowns were not even in the line-up. Such questionable decisions led to the formation of the British Showjumping Association [BSJA]. Countries held show-jumping competitions under their own rule; it was not until the formation of the Fédération Équestre Internationale (FEI) and many years on that all international competitions came under the same ruling in each country ...

... Courses, however, were built with little imagination. A common display would include two straight fences down each side of the arena with either a triple bar or water jump down the centre.

The idiosyncrasies of more faults for fore limbs were based on the values held in the hunting field where if a horse were to be careless with his front legs he would be more inclined to tip up and less so with the hind legs. Water jumps were a minimum 15ft in width though often the water had drained away by the time the last competitor had competed. High Jump would start with a single pole at a height of 5ft (1.52m) but this style of competition was abandoned due to horses commonly attempting the easier option of going under the pole rather than over and endangering the rider, therefore more poles had to be added to save noble heads.

In the early days the time element did not count and it was some years before a competitor was penalised for circling between obstacles.

In 1911 the International Horse Show received royal patronage and the King George V Gold Cup was awarded for the first time. In 1921 the FEI was formed and in 1923 the British Showjumping Association was formed with Lord Lonsdale as its first president. Lieutenant Colonel Charles (Taffy) Walwyn was appointed chairman and held the position for 15 years, was president from 1945 to 1956, and was then made honorary vice president. The appointed secretary was Phil Blackmore (who was later to become a course builder and designed the courses for the Victory Show at the White City in 1945). There were 197 Members of the Association when it was founded. In 1924 the BSJA membership increased to 277 Members and in 1925 the BSJA [now BS] was officially recognised as a company and incorporated in to the Companies Act.

ORIGINAL RULES IN 1925

Refusing or bolting at any fence	1st refusal	2 faults
	2nd refusal	3 faults
	3rd refusal	Debarment
Fall of horse, rider or both		4 faults
Horse touches the fence without knocking it down		½ fault
Horse upsets fence with:	Fore limbs	4 faults
	Hind limbs	2 faults
	Fore leg	2 faults
	Hind leg	1 fault
Upsetting or removing the water fence		½ fault

THE ARMY

Although it was a farmer who won that first Leaping Competition in Dublin, show jumping swiftly became a sport only for the army; it was thought to instil discipline and skill, as well as the quick-wittedness needed for instant decisions in war. Women were strictly prohibited from taking part.

The year 1932 saw the beginning of Irish supremacy in show jumping. Since the foundation of the Army Equitation School, the Irish Military teams grew from strength to strength. Until 1949 the Irish team remained the sole domain of military officers.

Cavalry regiments in particular took part in show jumping right across Europe up until the Second World War, by which time horses were no longer needed in war. Nations Cups were very much the preserve of cavalry officers until the mechanisation of the armies forced a change in the rules. Gradually, male civilian riders were accepted into the sport, and by the early 1950s it was only Italy and finally Ireland who still regularly produced army-only teams.

The Brief History of the [Irish] Army Equitation School states:

> The brave decision to form an Army Show Jumping team back in the infant days of the State in 1926 has been variously termed an ambitious undertaking, a foray into unknown territory,

a mission impossible. But perhaps the best comment on this far-reaching development at the time came from the French equestrian writer, Captain Montergon, when he declared, 'How fine the courage of the young Irish Army thus flinging itself boldly into the water in order to learn how to swim!'

Some eight years later this same author had changed his opinion. Writing in *Revue de Cavalerie*, he declared 'Ireland has indeed begun to swim and its swimming master Col Paul Rodzianko chose the proper method'. The master referred to there was the Russian riding instructor whose genius helped bring the new Irish team from the status of novice to one of the most feared squads in the world.

The formation of the Army Equitation School had come about very quickly in 1926 following contact between Judge Wylie of the RDS, Col Hogan (Quartermaster General), and the then head of the new Free State, President William T. Cosgrave. Through a miracle of far-sighted initiative, the funding was found to have Ireland field teams for international show jumping competitions. Its purpose – to advertise the new State and to promote the Irish horse, which in the long run would rebound to the benefit of farmer breeders around the country.

Recruitment began in early 1926. One of the first to be called, Ged O'Dwyer of Limerick, later declared, 'we were all hunting and racing men and knew nothing about show jumping'. Another recruit, Dan Corry of Galway, noted 'when we got to the barracks, the only horses there were pulling carts in the yard'.

In the ensuing years prior to the Second World War, the Irish Army team won twenty-three Nations Cups between 1928 and 1939. Among the team stalwarts were Cadet Jed O'Dwyer, Captain John Lewis, Captain Fred Ahern and Captain Dan Corry, while others who won for the Irish team in this time included Captain Cyril Harty, Captain Thomas Finlay, Captain Daniel Leonard, Commandant John Stack, Commandant George Heffernan, and Captain James Neylon.

In 1928 Cyril Harty was serving on the Curragh. In addition to being part of that first Irish team to win the Dublin Nations Cup, he also won the first show-jumping competition for Ireland as a Free State. He is better remembered for being part of the renowned Harty horse-racing family (he was the second of five generations). His son, Eddie, won the 1969 Aintree Grand National on Highland Wedding, and in recent times one of the top Irish racehorses was named after him, Captain Cee Bee, trained by his grandson, Eddie Harty Junior.

DID YOU KNOW?

When the Irish team of Dan Corry, Cyril Harty and Fred Ahern won the 1933 Toronto Nations Cup, a coin was tossed to decide the runner-up, giving second to Sweden ahead of the USA.

Traditionally, the previous year's winner at the Hickstead Derby will jump last, which has the advantage of the rider having noted how his rivals have fared and how the course is riding. History was made in 2012 when Paul Beecher became the first person to ever jump a clear round having been drawn to jump first in the competition. He then went on to win in a two-horse jump-off.

The first post-war Nations Cup in Dublin was won by Ireland, with the evergreen Dan Corry, John Stack and John Lewis steering their horses to yet another victory. Dan Corry won two more, in Dublin and in Harrisburg, in 1949, and he was still winning in Spain in 1951. In one class there, riding Ballycotton, he won after no fewer than five jump-offs, clearing seventy-five fences, and on the last day the pair won the Puissance (high jump); this consisted of a 6ft 1in stone wall, a double oxer of the same height with a wide spread, and a high jump of poles standing 6ft 4in.

Today, Puissance is associated with a high, red wall (not made of stone).

There is a story, told to me by Frank McGarry, that a few years later, in France, one of the Irish team riders, Roger Moloney, broke his leg shortly before he was due to ride in the main competition. As the ambulance was about to drive off with the injured rider, Colonel Dan Corry, who was by then team *chef d'équipe*, halted it, went inside and took the breeches, boots and tunic off Moloney and put them on himself. He hadn't competed for some while, but he went out and got on Moloney's horse, which he had never ridden before, and proceeded to jump two impeccable clear rounds.

Dan Corry had been a lynchpin of the (all-military) show-jumping team from 1928 (Dublin) right through until after the Second World

War; he was on the winning Nations Cup teams in Lucerne in 1931, Boston in 1932, Toronto in 1933, Lucerne, Dublin and New York in 1935, Nice, Amsterdam, Lucerne and Dublin in 1936, another three in 1937 including on home territory in Dublin, and an amazing Nice, Dublin, New York and Toronto in 1938. After the Second World War, Dan Corry was still there on winning teams: Dublin in 1946 and 1949, as well as Harrisburg that year. Pictures of him from the time show a neat, confident rider oozing horsemanship. He competed internationally for twenty-six years.

At the time there were many up-and-coming civilian riders, but they were not afforded international opportunities, which remained army-only. It also remained largely male-only; just one lady rider was allowed to represent Ireland once a year, in the Queen Elizabeth Ladies' Cup at White City.

The army horses were and still are kept and trained at the McKee Barracks in Dublin. Their usual route to the top went this way: they were bought as 'green' four-year-olds and taken hunting for a year before their serious schooling began. There could be up to seventy horses in the barracks at any given time, some of them thoroughbreds but the majority three-quarter-bred quality Irish hunters. The Irish Army show-jumping team competed internationally in cities such as New York, Washington and Toronto with success and became the envy of the rest of the world.

Pamela Macgregor-Morris tells a very Irish story in *The World's Show Jumpers*, published by Macdonald in 1955:

> The most sensational horse at Ballsbridge during the 1952 Dublin Show was a half-bred chestnut four-year-old called Lucky. Ridden by his owner, Jack Bamber, the well-known dealer from Ballymena, Northern Ireland – who has probably piloted more green horses safely round the course at Ballsbridge than any man living – Lucky jumped right through the show from Tuesday to Saturday, only faulting at the single bank.
>
> Lucky was bred in Cork, bought as an unbroken three-year-old at Cahirmee Fair by a Ballymena farmer, and sold to Jack Bamber in June 1952. Jack won with him at Clonmel and Navan, and then took him to Dublin. Until they saw him jump, few people in the jumping pocket wanted to buy him, for he is distinctly 'plain of himself'; but before the end of the week Jack was besieged by gentlemen bearing cheque books. The eventual purchasers were the Irish Army, who, understandably loath to see a potential champion escape from under their noses, paid, it is rumoured, considerably more than the Government-specified top price of £600 for this horse, for whom several English

buyers were prepared to go to four figures. When he arrived at McKee Barracks, where the Irish team horses are kept, Lucky was re-christened Glanmire.

In 1953, his first season with the Irish team, Glanmire was fortunate in being ridden by veteran Colonel Dan Corry, in the latter's last year with the team, and they placed in London and Dublin and won the Championship at Limerick.

In 1954, ridden by Lt. Brendan Cullinan, he went brilliantly at Dublin, winning the first International Event with the only clear round in the jump-off; dividing first with Voulette, on the second day: jumping two clear rounds on the third day, and one (in the Aga Khan Cup) on the fourth; and going clear until the last fence, where he fell, in the International Championship. His death in 1955 was a great loss to the Irish team.

Pamela Macgregor-Morris did not say what caused his death. Cahirmee Fair in Buttevant, County Cork is one of Europe's oldest horse fairs, and it is said that Napoleon's white charger Marengo and the Duke of Wellington's black horse Copenhagen, which he rode in the Battle of Waterloo, were both bought there. Buttevant is also known as the birthplace of steeplechasing following a match race across country from there to Doneraile in 1752.

In Britain, the constitution of the Army Equitation Association still states that: 'Equestrian sports are recognised army sports for which travel at public expense is authorised for a representative team.'

It also states:

Equestrian sports encourage or develop a) Good health, personal fitness and physical development; b) beneficial physical activity, especially for personnel in sedentary posts; c) self-discipline; d) high morale; e) coordination, competitiveness, determination, confidence and motivation; f) courage and character building; g) recruitment and retention in the Services.

Britain began using civilian riders much earlier than Ireland (Italy and Ireland were the last two nations to have a policy of army-only teams). While Pamela Macgregor-Morris had described six horses owned by the Irish Army in her *The World's Show Jumpers*, and two of the further six had army connections, none of the sixteen horses she described as representing Great Britain were owned by the army and only two had military connections, Colonel Sir Harry Llewellyn's mighty Foxhunter, and Major G.B. Gibbon's Blue Lady. The 16.3½hh Irish mare was also ridden by her owner and together they won the Officers' Jumping at

Aldershot. She represented Britain in Rotterdam where she won two classes and was part of the winning British Nations Cup team.

Geoffrey Gibbon had already shown his ability before Blue Lady came along. He won a number of British Army on the Rhine (BAOR) classes on a mare called Sarah, including Grand Prix in Rotterdam and Baden Baden; he was also successful with another mare, his speed horse called Saida. She was a grey Belgium Anglo-Arab standing just 15.2hh who had won a lot in Belgium when Geoffrey Gibbon bought her; he then won the Puissance in Berlin, classes in Ghent and Paris and, at Harringay in 1954, teamed up with Lady Mary Rose Williams and Grey Skies to win the International Pair Relay. The next year she won the Blarney Cup in Cork, beating Nizefela and Wilf White on time. He then captained the 1955 British team in Paris, and at the Rhine Army Show in Aachen.

Foxhunter's name lives on today, not only in the memory of the older generation but as the nation-wide Foxhunter class for novice show jumpers with its sought-after final at the Horse of the Year Show.

DID YOU KNOW?

Eddie Macken, Harvey Smith, John Whitaker and Michael Whitaker have won the Hickstead Derby four times in its long history, but only Eddie Macken has achieved this feat on the same horse, Boomerang, and in consecutive years in the 1970s.

Sir Harry Llewellyn's great horse Foxhunter helped Britain to its first Olympic gold medal for show jumping at Helsinki in 1952. He also won the King George V Gold Cup three times and was in twelve winning Nations Cups teams. It is said that Sir Harry initially donated the Foxhunter competition cups as a means of giving away his many trophies because his wife did not want to clean them.

He was bred in Norfolk in 1940 by a thoroughbred out of a brilliant half-Clydesdale hunting mare called Catcall. Foxhunter had two educational seasons hunting with the Quorn – he was also a dab hand at jumping in and out of his barn and over ditches in his field.

Harry Llewellyn bought him in 1947 after, it was said, scouring the records of the BSJA for a promising jumper (so he must have done some classes in addition to hunting.) Once Foxhunter was with Colonel Llewellyn the pair became household names, winning a total of seventy-eight international competitions together. Moreover, they were part of the gold-medal winning team at the 1952 Olympic Games in Helsinki.

Foxhunter died at the Colonel's home in Abergavenny aged 19, and was buried on a nearby mountain. Forty years later, in 1999, Colonel Llewellyn's ashes were scattered around the memorial.

NATIONS CUPS

The first Nations Cup, held at Olympia, London, in 1909 was open to 'teams of three officers of the same nationality in uniform.'

The winners were to hold the King Edward VII Gold Cup, valued at £500, for one year; the runners-up received a Reserve Ribbon. From the start the event was well supported, and that first year saw teams competing from three continents. It was won by France, with Italy second and Great Britain third, followed by Canada, Belgium and Argentina.

The cup, made by the Goldsmiths and Silversmiths Company of Regent Street, London, was won outright by the Russians in 1914, and was replaced by the Edward Prince of Wales Cup.

Those early Nations Cups were over two rounds of the same course, just as they are today, but almost all were open only to officers, with all three scores to count. Gradually, civilian gentlemen were allowed to participate, and teams of four were allowed to compete, with the score of the horse with the most faults being discarded; today, the worst score can be discarded in both rounds, whether or not it is the same horse.

Originally, also, if a nation could not field three riders, one member could ride twice, on two different horses; the team riders jumped one after the other, but today the method is to take one member from each team in turn, as drawn in advance. Currently, for the second round anticipation is heightened by having the teams jump in reverse order of merit, with the lowest first round score jumping last, and so on, leading to an exciting climax. In the event of equality after the two rounds a jump-off is held.

Every country may hold just one Nations Cup in a year, except for a country as large as the USA which can run three. Since 2013 the world of show jumping has been divided into six regions: Europe 1; Europe 2; North and Central American and Caribbean; South America; Middle East; and Africa. The best of each region, on a cumulative points system, qualifies for the world final. In that final, the top four riders from the first two rounds then jump again on all three of the other riders' horses, making a unique championship test.

Great Britain won its first Nations Cup in 1921 on home territory with Geoffrey Brooke, Malise Graham and H.G. Morrison; it followed up the following year, also in London, with Malise Graham, C.T. 'Taffy' Walwyn and J.H. Gibbon, and again in 1924 and 1926 (Italy won both the intervening London legs), and for four years from 1927 to 1930.

Ireland first staged a Nations Cup in Dublin in 1926, the year it became a Free State. It was won in the first two years by Switzerland, but in 1928 Ireland took it for the first time, with Dan Corry, Jed O'Dwyer and Cyril Harty. In 1932 the Irish won on home ground again, with Jed O'Dwyer, Fred Ahern and Daniel Leonard. Ireland went through a golden patch with three successive wins from 1977 to 1979 in Dublin with the team of Eddie Macken, Paul Darragh, Con Power and James Kernan. Ireland won again in 2004, 2012 and 2015.

With Nations Cups held throughout Europe, America and beyond, both Britain and Ireland have also won many competitions away from home.

COLONEL SIR MICHAEL ANSELL

It was while languishing in a prisoner-of-war camp during the Second World War that Colonel (later Sir) Michael Ansell dreamed up and planned the future expansion and magnetism of show jumping. Taken prisoner after 'friendly' fire left him blinded for life, after the war Mike Ansell truly became Mr Show Jumping. He possessed army discipline combined with vision (regardless of his blindness) and aptitude to turn it into a world sport. It was he who foresaw that it was a natural choice for television.

Mike Ansell died in 1994 and it was his fellow 5th Inniskilling Dragoon Guards comrade General Sir Cecil 'Monkey' Blacker who wrote this obituary for the *Daily Telegraph* on 2 March 1994:

Michael Picton Ansell, show-jumping administrator: born The Curragh, Co Kildare 26 March 1905; DSO 1944; Chairman, British Showjumping Association 1945–64, 1970–71, President 1964–66; Show Director, Royal International Horse of the Year Show 1949–75; CBE 1951; Kt 1968; President/Chairman British Equestrian Federation 1972–76; President, St Dunstan's

1977–86; married 1936 Victoria Fuller (died 1969; two sons, one daughter), 1970 Eileen Evans (*née* Stanton, died 1971); died Brighton 17 February 1994.

Michael Ansell was an outstanding leader of equestrian sport in Britain, and former chairman of both the British Equestrian Federation and the British Show Jumping Association.

By the middle 1930s, as a young cavalry officer in the 5th Inniskilling Dragoon Guards, Ansell had already shown himself not only an exceptional and inspirational commander but an international show jumper and polo player – one of the army's rising stars. After war broke out he became the youngest commanding officer in the British Army when he took command in March 1940, at the age of 35, of the 1st Lothian and Border Yeomanry in France. Then the string of unbroken triumphs was fractured and changed to one of personal disaster.

The Lothians were attached to the 51st Highland Division, and during the fighting before the retreat to St Valery Ansell won the DSO. On arrival in the town the division found no ships on which to embark, and the divisional commander ordered surrender. Determined to escape, Ansell and a few companions took shelter for the night in the loft of a barn. A party of English soldiers later entered the barn and, believing the occupants above them to be Germans, discharged a hail of fire upwards.

Ansell, blinded and severely wounded in the hand, was taken prisoner and underwent agonising and prolonged treatment in unavailing efforts to save his eyes, and spent the next three years in a prisoner-of-war camp. It was during those years that he began to put together his ideas about promoting equestrianism as a spectator sport after the war.

Repatriated in 1943, he took up horticulture and, typically, was soon winning prizes. Then one day he was asked to become chairman of the British Show Jumping Association. Still in his early forties, and with personal international experience, Ansell proceeded to transform the sport's public image.

As far as possible he acted as if he were not blind at all, and talked quite naturally about 'seeing' people, or 'watching' competitions. He developed a formidable memory and an uncanny way of sensing what was going on around him. He grasped every opportunity to promote equestrian sport. He also realised that the way to public recognition and applause was through international success.

He restarted the Royal International Horse Show, moving it from Olympia to White City. By the 1950s it attracted audiences of 80,000 people (numbers were boosted after Britain won the team gold medal at the 1952 Helsinki Olympics). A new venture, and an almost immediate success, was the Horse of the Year Show, first at Haringey and later transferred to Wembley. Ansell insisted, against much opposition, that Britain should enter a Three Day Event team in the Wembley 1948 Olympics. Although Britain won no medals, the Duke of Beaufort was sufficiently impressed to offer Badminton, in Gloucestershire, as a future venue for the sport. This has become the finest event of its kind in the world, and British teams were soon winning Olympic medals in eventing as well.

Tall, erect and spare, Mike Ansell emanated personality in waves. He so dominated the equestrian world that for nearly twenty years he virtually decided everything: his word was law and his personality demolished all opposition. In the international as well as the domestic equestrian scene he became a senior and influential figure. 'Colonel Mike' generated such enthusiasm and confidence that, with him in charge, any enterprise would succeed.

In 1970, his wife Victoria died after a slow and painful illness, and nine months later he married Eileen Evans, the widow of his pre-war commanding officer. Six months after that Eileen was killed by a lorry which mounted the pavement on which she was walking. Even Ansell's iron determination wilted under that cruel blow.

Mike Ansell's interests were by no means confined to the horse. He loved flowers, and he was a successful salmon fisherman, despite his disability. He was always deeply grateful to St Dunstan's, the society for soldiers blinded in action, and proud to be its president from 1977 to 1986.

UNITING IRELAND

In the early 1950s the Irish show-jumping team for international competitions came from the army and civilians were still not invited to represent their country. In this pre-television era, shows were a great local attraction at weekends; a big day out for city dwellers and farmers alike. If the army could be persuaded to send competitors, the crowds were certain to flock in.

As Judith Draper says in *Show Jumping, Records, Facts and Champions*:

There were very few rules and regulations in Irish show-jumping of the early 1950s, and there were no timed jump-offs (in which the fastest second round with the fewest faults is declared the winner, from those who achieved an initial clear round). With no timed jump off, classes would go on for perhaps as many as six rounds until one horse alone cleared the course that had been heightened for each round; banks and natural stone walls were normal features in Irish competitions. The judging process in Ireland was wrought with inconsistencies; for instance, the wall was topped by pebbles, and if they were knocked off by two front feet the horse was penalised with four faults, but if some were knocked off by his hind feet this resulted in two faults.

It was not always possible for a judge to see exactly what a horse's feet were doing; in muddy ground, for instance, a flying sod could be mistaken for a stone. Judith Draper notes, 'Prior to the standardization of rules, fence judges did not have an easy time, particularly in Ireland'. *Horse and Hound* of 17 August 1946 has this to say about the Dublin Show:

> In Military competitions 4 faults are counted if the obstacle is knocked with either front or hind legs, except in the case of the wall, where one fault is recorded if up to three stones are dislodged by the hind legs, and two if dislodged by the front legs. There are further penalties if more stones are dislodged ... Six different mistakes can be penalized over the single bank, including changing leg on the top. There are six for the double bank, too, and in this case the horse is faulted if he does *not* change!

The first meeting of the Irish Show Jumping Association took place in 1952 in the Vocational School Tobercurry, County Sligo with the intention of forming the Irish Show Jumping Association (ISJA) along the lines of Northern Ireland and Britain. The secretaries of most Irish shows in the West attended the initial meeting. They listened to those from the North who had a well-regulated set of rules already. In the Republic, at that time, faults in show jumping were given as 1, 2, 3, and 4; by taking on the same rules as Northern Ireland there would be a unilateral three faults for a refusal, four faults for a knock down of a fence, three refusals elimination, eight faults for a fall – which was the worldwide accepted code for many years.

Sligo show-jumping enthusiast and horse owner Frank McGarry played a big role in the reforms of the 1950s. He pushed for Irish civilians to be allowed to represent their country as also for the North to be included in the Irish team, arguing that it would strengthen Irish show jumping.

There were a number of riders from the North who were good enough to jump internationally, but the UK had the strength in depth to produce three teams if it wished, while Ireland struggled to raise one, even though Irish riders gained extra experience by regularly jumping on the British circuit. The talented riders in the North then and in later years included Jessica Chesney (Kurten), James Kiernan, Harry Marshall, Dermot Lennon, Billy McCully, Brian Henry and John Brooke.

Initial negotiations took six years. There were advantages for both North and South. The South could avail of the talent in the North, and the North, being a part of the United Kingdom, was up against riders from Scotland, Wales and England for selection. If those from the North rode for one Ireland they would have more chance of being selected.

Frank McGarry found backing from Judge John Wiley, who was on the executive committee of the RDS and the Equestrian Federation of Ireland. In 1956 the amalgamation was agreed to but there followed another two years of seemingly endless meetings to iron out the problems of the flag. The North wouldn't jump under the tricolour and the Republic wouldn't have national representation without it.

In the green, white and orange vertical sections of the tricolour, the green represents the nationalism of a united island of Ireland, the orange reflects the majority tradition in the North, populated by settlers who were originally 'planted' from Britain and whose King William of Orange beat the deposed King James II at the Battle of the Boyne in 1690, while the white of peace rests between them, a laudable and, one would have hoped, appropriate premise.

At last, in 1958, a compromise was reached: it was agreed to use a Four Provinces Flag, consisting of emblems that stood for each province, and matching saddle cloths. (The province of Ulster, often referred to meaning Northern Ireland, also has three counties in the Republic: Cavan, Monaghan and, furthest north, Donegal.)

An all-Ireland team to jump abroad now appeared ready to go – but there remained another problem: which National Anthem to use. No Northern person, it was said, would stand under the tricolour or listen to 'The Soldier's Song' being played. In one blow, it appeared that the years of discussions had been for nothing, and they started all over again.

This took another two years of sometimes tortuous debates. Finally, the Four Provinces Flag and saddle cloths were again agreed upon for international competitions, with the exception of Nations Cups, for which the tricolour flag and saddle cloths would be used.

Next for the anthem. It was this issue that brought more problems than the flag. Eventually, the anthem chosen was 'St Patrick's Day Parade', and, for Nations Cups, 'The Soldier's Song'.

The army, when they jumped as a team, looked smart in their uniforms; most Irish civilian riders wore black, red or even grey jackets, and before long it was decided that the civilians should jump in the green jackets that remain an iconic feature of Irish international show jumping today.

One civilian team of Leslie Fitzpatrick, Tommy Brennan, Tommy Wade and John Brooke with Omar Van Lanegan as *chef d'équipe* had already been invited abroad a year or two earlier, but before the green jackets were universally used.

John Brooke was son of Northern Ireland's third Prime Minister, Sir Basil Brooke, 1st Viscount Brookborough. John faced a dilemma about jumping under the tricolour: it would mean, if the team won, standing to attention under the flag to the National Anthem of another country to that of which his father was premier, and in the end he only went once on a team; subsequently he retired completely from international competition.

BETTING IN SHOW JUMPING

While horse racing was, for a long time, the traditional betting forum, it has come to take a back seat with the advent of online betting and the betting-on-almost-anything culture.

Although one does not tend to see rows of bookmakers' boards at show-jumping events, it is something that has been recorded since about the 1940s. Pat Smythe recalled it taking place at Madrid Show in the 1940s and I can remember Douglas Bunn introducing it to Hickstead in the 1970s.

Much more recently, in early June 2015, Robert Fagan staged the last qualifier and the final of a €20,000 Bet Show-jumping Live 1.30m competition complete with on-site and in-shop betting at the International Show at his Mullingar Equestrian Centre, Mullingar, County Westmeath.

It was a knock-out class that was exciting for spectators to watch, while the prize money ensured it would be well contested. Earlier qualifying rounds had been held at Millstreet, Louth and Galway, giving a broad spread across the country. Each was run to a similar design to encourage consistency. Eight riders from each show, including

Mullingar, brought thirty-two riders through to the final. These were then divided into four groups of eight who jumped off against each other, with the winner of each going forward to the four-horse final, and the prize money was divided among the finalists.

After each octet had competed there was a break to allow betting to take place on the next round. A form sheet, similar to a racecard, was produced for the final.

Robert Fagan plans for his Olympic-sized outside arena complex to be finished in time for his 2016 feature event. It was used in 2015 but by 2016 it will also have a new international stable block, a hospitality pavilion and a bigger trade village.

The new betting competition was encouraged by Horse Sport Ireland. Patrick McCartan, Equestrian Sport Consultant, said, ' Paddy Power, our partner in the Bet ShowJumping Live competition, were very encouraged by the interest shown by their clientele on this, the first opportunity to bet on show jumping through their offices. Most of the bets placed could be traced to those with a direct involvement in the competition – owners, riders, grooms or family members of the competitors.

The favourite at the start of the competition was English visitor Emily Ward riding King Mac at a price of 7/2. Irish riders Emily Turkington on Legend and Nicola Fitzgibbon riding Lady Georgina Forbes' Castleforbes Tina were joint second favourites at 9/2 with experienced duo Francis Connors on Uskerty Diamond Lady and Seamus Hayes riding Twister at an attractive 8/1.

Winners of the four groups and final four competitors were: Nicola Fitzgibbon with Castleforbes, Tina Francis Connors with Uskerty Diamond Lady, Kenneth Graham with Lenamore Donatella and Gerard Clarke with Zanzibar V.

In a great jump-off the experience and guile of the Waterford rider was crucial and he left all the fences standing in a very fast time to seal a famous victory.'

It was really a new innovation from Robert, to generate more popular interest in the sport.

1st Francis Connors with Uskerty Diamond Lady	€10,000
2nd Gerard Clarke with Zanzibar V	€5,000
3rd Nicola Fitzgibbon with Castleforbes Tina	€3,000
4th Kenneth Graham with Lenamore Donatella	€2,000

2
VENUES

ALL-ENGLAND JUMPING
COURSE, HICKSTEAD, SUSSEX

The brainchild of the charismatic entrepreneur Douglas Bunn in 1960, Hickstead has rightly become one of the world's top equestrian venues, known in particular for its annual Hickstead Derby. Set between Gatwick Airport and the regency seaside town of Brighton, Hickstead today is also the home of the Royal International Horse Show.

Duggie Bunn, a leap-year baby born in 1928, was far from a one-trick pony, and was well able to combine business with pleasure, especially show jumping and hunting. By 1959, he could see that Great Britain was being outstripped in terms of imaginative show-jumping courses both in Europe and America. With typical gusto, he set about putting on 'the best show jumping possible anywhere in the world'. Only one year later, the All-England Jumping Course at Hickstead was born, and the Derby one year after that.

In his leisure time, Bunn loved following the Mid Surrey Farmers Draghounds, of which he was a joint-master from 1976 to 2000; he relished the big, challenging hedges on his own farmland that surrounds the show-jumping site. It was here, with the Easter show-jumping meeting needing an injection of excitement, that he came up with the concept of team chasing; he was having lunch with the BBC's sports producer Alan Mouncer, and he jotted down the proposed format on the back of a menu. What followed was the inaugural invitation-only event on Good Friday 1974. The exploits of the twenty teams were recorded by the BBC television cameras; the teams were made up of show jumpers, jockeys, event riders and dressage riders and included a racing journalists team (John Oaksey, Brough Scott, Robin Gray and the author) and the Mid Surrey Farmers Draghounds team. And so the new sport was born, enjoyed today all over Great Britain with an annual championship, run over two miles of daunting mostly natural country, the fastest team being the winners. One of the features of the sport is its relative lack of rules, which makes it quite simplistic – in theory; the daunting part comes in the actual cross-country challenge.

Today, most fixtures include classes over a smaller course and run to a 'bogey' optimum time that is not known in advance.

An early and enduring stalwart was George Goring, whose Goring Hotel, London sponsored the National Team Chase Championships for twenty years until 2013 when he finally retired, aged 74: he was a member of Duggie Bunn's own team every year until the Easter Hickstead meeting gave way to a later one at Whitsun in 1982.

Duggie Bunn was a man who lived life to the full, and he will always be principally remembered for the Hickstead Derby.

The Derby, first held in 1961 when Hickstead was just a year old, provides the ultimate show-jumping test of horse and rider; at 1,995m in length it is exceptionally long for a show-jumping class. The inspiration for the Derby bank came from Hamburg, which had begun its gruelling and challenging Derby back in 1920. The story goes, say Hickstead, that Douglas Bunn had seen film footage of the Hamburg Derby and decided to visit the German showground to measure the bank and replicate it back home in West Sussex. He arrived on New Year's Eve when it was snowing, and went round the showground measuring fences – much to the bemusement of the show's officials. The layer of snow on top of the Hamburg bank must have affected Douglas's measurements, as Hickstead's bank stands 6in taller than its German counterpart. The rails at the bottom of the Hickstead Derby bank are two strides away from the bottom of the bank, but the Hamburg Derby bank's equivalent upright stands just one stride away.

Other fences that Bunn built on his attractive mid-Sussex venue were a double of water ditches, the Road Jump and the Devil's Dyke. The latter is named after a well-known canyon-like geographical feature on the nearby South Downs, familiar to walkers and riders. These are permanent fences and they gave British show jumpers the chance to jump the sort of fences that they were encountering on the Continent.

The first fence is a stone wall standing 4ft 8in high with a single pole on top of it, positioned in the middle of the ring and known as The Cornishman. It is relatively easy but nevertheless gets its share of faulters. There are five fences which stand at 5ft 3in and three fences are 6ft 6in wide.

The three-part Devil's Dyke, while not the biggest fence, often proves the trickiest. The water jump was originally 16ft wide and was the first permanent Olympic-sized water jump to be built in Britain. It now measures 15ft wide and has been made shallower – the water used to be knee-level.

The Derby Rails (fence 12) are based along some rails Douglas saw when driving along the Bagshot Bypass. He decided they'd make a good show jump – so he stopped his car to measure the railings and then made a replica at Hickstead.

While the fences still look like the same solid, daunting jumps they always were, the top rails have all been switched to lightweight versions (which fall more easily!), while safety cups are used as well.

There are several gates in the Derby course because Douglas Bunn wanted to include fences that people could identify with – they'd know how big a five-bar gate is and could appreciate its size, compared to just endless coloured poles.

The year 2015 saw the fifty-fifth running of the Hickstead Derby; up until then only fifty-six clear rounds had been achieved in its first fifty-four years. There have been eighteen years without a clear at all, and on just three occasions, three horses have each achieved a clear round.

The first winner was Irish rider Seamus Hayes on Goodbye, and they won again in 1964. David Broome jumped clear in 1963 but had a fall on the flat with Mister Softee, which incurred faults, leaving victory to the great Brazilian rider Nelson Pessoa. He had to wait for his trophy, however, as it had been stolen from a shop window in London.

Pessoa repeated his victory in 1965 and then, incredibly, after a gap of thirty-one years, he won again, in 1996, on the 19-year-old Loro Piana Vivaldi. Nelson Pessoa was 60 years old, had suffered a heart attack the previous November, and was wearing a heart monitor during his ride.

Stroller jumped a total of three clear rounds, yet only won once, in 1967; he also placed three times. Harvey Smith, brothers John and Michael Whitaker and Eddie Macken all won the class four times, but Macken's feat was to achieve this in succession on the inimitable Boomerang from 1976 to 1979.

Smith won with Mattie Brown in 1970, then forgot to return the trophy the next year, to Douglas Bunn's annoyance; Smith won the class again that year, 1971, prompting his infamous two-fingered gesture to the Master of Hickstead, as Bunn was known. Initially Smith was disqualified, but in time his prize was reinstated.

German ace rider Paul Schockemöhle won the event three times in the 1980s, twice with the mighty Deister, and Nick Skelton also won it three times in the same decade, twice with Apollo. Michael Whitaker notched up a treble in the early 1990s, all three times with Mon Santa, and a decade later Peter Charles did exactly the same with Corrada. William Funnell won it three times in four years with Cortaflex Mondrian. Kilbaha only won once, but he notched clear rounds in three successive years for John Ledingham in the 1990s.

Paul Beecher made history in 2012 by being the first ever person to jump a clear round when drawn to go first in the competition, and he went on to win it.

Douglas Bunn was chairman of the British Showjumping Association from 1993 to 1995, and president from 2001 to 2004. Bunn died in 2009, but his legacy lives on. Six of his nine children are at the helm (two of them, Edward and Lizzie, full time) and they follow his traditions while continually making improvements and refurbishments. Another son, John, is MD of the other family business, Bunn Leisure, while daughter Chloe is based at Hickstead with her husband, show-jumper Shane Breen. Their celebrations must have been memorable when Shane's brother Trevor won the 2014 Hickstead Derby with the one-eyed Adventure De Kannan – as they were, too, when Hickstead celebrated its fiftieth anniversary in 2010. Among the highlights was a letter of congratulations from the Queen.

Today, a number of jumping derbies have proliferated around the world.

Apart from the annual Derby, Hickstead has also hosted top championships, including European and Junior European

DID YOU KNOW?

The great show-jumper Boomerang was originally called Battle Boy. Later in his career he was registered as Carroll's Boomerang, in deference to his sponsors.

Dundrum originally pulled a luggage cart from the station in Tipperary to local hotels. The diminutive horse was sold to Tommy Wade with whom he reached world show-jumping stardom. He stood only 15 hands high, but won International Grand Prix, speed classes and Puissance and became, and remains, an all-time favourite. In 1961 Dundrum became Supreme Champion at Wembley Horse of the Year Show, when he cleared a 7ft 2in Puissance wall. He made sporting history by winning five major events in the Dublin Horse Show and not surprisingly he became Ireland's hero. No wonder he did not prove an ideal cart horse!

Championships, the World Championships and, since 1971, the Great Britain Nations Cup. This is part of the Royal International Horse Show which moved to Hickstead in 1992.

On a different level, Hickstead is also home to the annual Inter-Schools Competition, and this used to be one of my favourite days of the year. The excitement was almost tangible and the occasion was choreographed superbly, as I'm sure it still is. Today it is combined with the Pony Club Championships.

Nowadays there are six arenas in use, and although the team chase has long ceased on the surrounding land, Hickstead has staged top-class dressage since 1996, and ten years later it opened the All-England Polo Club, which takes place through the winter months. For good measure, Hickstead has also become a wedding venue.

ARENA UK

In the East of England, Arena UK at Willow Top Farm, Allington, near Grantham in Lincolnshire, plays host to many British show jumping regional and national championships on its 515 acre site not far from the A1.

Regular British dressage events are held, and it is also home to the British Show Pony Society National Showing Championships.

Arena UK boasts the UK's largest outdoor all-weather surface arena, coupled with a spacious indoor arena, warm-up area, covered collecting ring, ring-side restaurant and dedicated hospitality areas. It holds events throughout the year for all levels and ages, from training to unaffiliated classes right up to the top flight; in recent times it has opened itself to the public on non-show days. Demonstrations by top riders also feature throughout the year.

Its annual highlight is its UK Festival of Show Jumping in September, which features the UK's largest national championship, with a prize fund of £120,000. Its Grand Prix is worth £45,000, with £15,000 to the winner: at the time of writing, this is the biggest first prize in Britain. Other big events in this show are the Puissance and the Young Rider class.

Its Indoor main arena, coupled with two permanent marquee structures and hard-standing for over 800 vehicles, offers the perfect location for trade fairs, product launches and exhibitions. Arena UK also has over 200 acres of grass fields available for outdoor events.

BICTON

The south west is renowned for its scenery, and there would be few more beautiful settings for an equestrian venue than that in glorious parkland at Bicton, Devon. It is also accessible, being not far from the M5.

Apart from its premier grass arena, Bicton also has two all-weather arenas, in addition to another five competition rings. It is more than just show jumping; it also has a cross-country course with a choice of more than 100 fences.

Dressage also takes place there, and it is a favourite venue for Pony Club and adult camps alike. Clinics, lecture demonstrations, training days and unaffiliated competitions are equally popular.

OLYMPIA

For anyone with even a passing interest in horses, and especially pony-mad children, there is no better way to get into the Christmas spirit than by visiting the annual London International Horse Show, Olympia in about the third week of December.

The atmosphere is infectious, and after you have been once it will easily become an annual imperative. It is not only about show jumping, which is of the top class, but it is also about special displays, a magical finale to each session, retail therapy for those last-minute Christmas gifts, and international dressage as well. The Shetland Pony Grand National is always a crowd puller, and driving and dog-agility classes add to the excitement.

Star-struck children will be able to see their show-jumping idols close up, and maybe secure a few autographs. The highlights of the show jumping include Puissance, where the wall gets ever higher as the horses left get fewer, and the Grand Prix.

The original Olympia building, with its 170ft high clear roof span, was opened on Boxing Day 1886. Two years later, with show jumping in its infancy, the First Great Horse Show was held, which has since morphed into the international show of today. Since then, Olympia has hosted many and varied events, including the Ideal Home Show, the Boat Show, the Cycle and Motor Cycle Show, the National Poultry Show (post war), and, in 1958, the first British Electronic Computer Exhibition. Various pop stars have performed there, and in 1967 it became home to Crufts Dog Show. The Olympia of today is a high-powered business and conference centre – but for show-jumping fans it means one thing: the International Horse Show at Christmas.

HORSE HUMOUR

My daughter has taken up show jumping and is really very good at it.
In fact, I can't fault her.
(Courtesy of Sickipedia.org)

MILLSTREET, COUNTY CORK

From little acorns big oak trees grow. When Noel C. Duggan founded his equestrian centre at his home, Green Glens in Millstreet, near Duhallow in County Cork, in 1973, he had ambitions – but even he might not then have realised that by 2015, it would boast sixteen outdoor arenas (eight for competitions and eight for warming up), three indoor arenas and stabling for about 1,500 horses. It also has parking for 1,000 horseboxes and sites for 200 caravans and motor homes.

Millstreet Horse Show in August is Ireland's largest annual equestrian event. It follows on from the RDS Show in Dublin and lasts for seven days, becoming in the process a shop window for the Irish equestrian industry; as such, young-horse classes feature strongly. These include the Young Irelander loose jumping for three-year-old horses and the National Discovery for four-year-olds. More recently there is also the National Eventing Discovery class. All age levels and grades are catered for with a full range of national classes as well as Ireland's richest Pony Grand Prix with a prize fund of €4,500.

The week-long show is held in the second week of August each year, and many international stars extend their stay to take in the Cork event. It runs the only Irish CSI class, and in 2014 it offered a total prize fund exceeding €180,000.

It is not just show jumping that has kept visitors enthralled over the years. In 1993 Millstreet hosted the Eurovision Song Contest, Ireland having won the previous year; Ireland promptly won it again.

Noel gave the venue for free but it was a canny move, because many of the local roads and amenities had to be improved to cater for the arrival of the international entourages – and this in turn led to good access permanently to his showground in future years.

Nor is that the only non-equestrian event to have been staged at Millstreet. The County Cork venue has also seen world-class boxing contests, international juggling conventions, and pop concerts.

Steve Collins twice successfully defended his super middleweight World Boxing Organization (WBO) title in Millstreet, beating Chris Eubank in 1995, and Neville Brown in 1996. Millstreet also hosted the European Juggling Convention in July 2006 and July 2014 and artists such as The Prodigy, James Blunt and Westlife have performed there. By contrast, but in keeping with its rural surroundings, in 2007 it hosted the John Deere show, in which Deere & Company unveiled new agricultural machinery. It also hosted the Farm Machinery Show in January 2008 and 2009. In addition it has accommodated Disney on Ice and many conventions, political or otherwise.

DID YOU KNOW?

Only two mares have won the Hickstead Derby in its 54-year history. The first to win the title was John Popely's Bluebird, who was having her fifth attempt in the class in 1996. She was joined soon after by Corrada, who didn't touch a pole during any of her three wins (2001–2003) with Peter Charles – although she did get time faults in 2001 for starting three seconds late.

John Whitaker's second win came in 1998, when he finished top on the 21-year-old Gammon, who remains the oldest horse to win the Hickstead Derby. Two years later, John won on Welham, who was 20. That was his second attempt at the Hickstead Derby, after finishing second in 1995. John and the 20-year-old gelding joined Rob Hoesktra (on Lionel) and Tim Stockdale (on Wiston Bridget) in a three-way jump-off, with the veteran gelding netting the fastest time to give John his third Derby title.

3

RIDERS

BERTRAM ALLEN

At just 19 years old the young Irishman Bertram Allen finished a nail-bitingly close third for the title of World Champion in 2015.

In amongst the glitz and hype of Las Vegas he remained cool, calm and collected. And remember, this is not just a one-horse event, so it does not matter that Allen has an outstanding horse in the mare Molly Molone, for this is the championship in which after two days the top four riders have to jump all three of their rivals' horses. They are allowed only a matter of minutes in which to warm up and acquaint themselves with the feel and possible idiosyncrasies of the horse beneath them.

As I write (in 2015), young Bertram Allen is making the show-jumping headlines week after week. His progress towards his world-title attempt was well chronicled in Ireland's weekly *The Irish Field*, and the following article portrays not only his successes leading up to it but also how the show-jumping circuit works at the highest level. It describes the Irish disappointment of failing to qualify for next year's Olympic Games in spite of having three riders in the top twelve at their last event, and it takes a peek at some of Bertram's inner thoughts, giving a glimpse of what sacrifices he has made to achieve his dream, not least leaving home at sixteen to live and train in Germany:

> While 2014 saw some incredible performances on the world stage by a number of international riders, it will be remembered without doubt as the year that a new young Irish super star introduced himself to the world, with some quite extraordinary displays of raw talent.
>
> 19-year-old Bertram Allen from Enniscorthy, Co Wexford, was no stranger to equestrian fans here in Ireland after enjoying an incredible pony career which saw him claim numerous team and individual medals at European level, including individual gold in 2010 at Bishop Burton in England with Acapalla Z.

Allen went on to win the European junior individual gold in 2012 with Wild Thing and individual silver the following year but few could have expected that his senior jumping career would begin in quite such a dramatic fashion.

The quietly spoken teenager's incredible run of 2014 results began at Lummen in Belgium last April with a win in the €50,000 Longines Grand Prix.

Speaking to *The Irish Field* during a short trip home to Co Wexford over Christmas, Bertram looked back on his incredible season.

'It was a dream year, Lummen really kick-started everything, Molly Malone had done some big Grands Prix before that, but that was her first Nations Cup appearance and we jumped a four and clear in the cup. I had jumped a few promotional league Nations Cups the year before but that was our first Super-League appearance.'

When asked about his memories of the Grand Prix win at Lummen, Allen quickly remarked: 'I remember every bit of it. It was jumped over three rounds and five of us went through to the jump-off where I was second last to go. The year before Molly Malone was a bit behind Romonov in terms of performance but in 2014 Molly really stepped up, she has a great gallop and really covers the ground.'

Bertram scored several more International wins as the season continued but even at this young age, he quite obviously has a special regard for being part of the Irish team and has already been bitten by the bug of competing in a Nations Cup for his country.

'Hickstead was the first points-scoring round that I jumped on and we finished third, I didn't jump Molly Malone in the Grand Prix at Hickstead as I was saving her for Dublin the week after so I went with Romonov in the Grand Prix instead, he seemed to love the big open grass arena in Hickstead and I was delighted to finish second in the Gold Cup behind Beezie Madden.'

Allen's mount Romonov was previously ridden by Billy Twomey and despite that Corkman's undoubted talents, many people believe that Romonov jumps much better for Bertram, who when asked about this replied: 'I don't really know why, we just seem to get on really well together and he has been very lucky for me.'

A week after Hickstead, Bertram Allen would become the second youngest rider in history to jump on an Aga Khan team in Dublin, second only to James Kiernan.

We asked him when exactly he got the news that he would be part of the five-man team for Ireland's biggest jumping event.

'I was told by Robert Splaine during the show at Rotterdam in June that I would be on the Aga Khan squad for Dublin so it helped a lot to have that time to prepare. I eased up a bit beforehand with Molly and just did one show in a month.'

Speaking about the build-up to Aga Khan Friday, Bertram, whose family are former owners of Bewleys Hotel which overlooks the Simmonscourt Arena at the RDS, said: 'From the minute you arrive at the show as a member of the Aga Khan squad, it is just completely different than being there as an individual. For an Irish rider it is just the best show in the world, but to be one of the five riders on the team is special. Then as part of the build-up, you have all the speculation as to who will be on the team and who will miss out.

'The day itself is just what you live for, it's such a special atmosphere. Three years before, I was jumping there in the pony competitions and I remember trying to squeeze in and find somewhere to watch the Nations Cup on the Friday.'

Was he nervous facing such a daunting task in front of his home fans?

'I quite liked the whole occasion, in Dublin when you trot into the ring and the whole place erupts, it feels like you are on a football or rugby pitch. It's a special feeling that you don't really get at any other venue in the world and even the foreign riders say that too, everyone gets a cheer. Then you need to settle yourself down and you can really enjoy it after you jump the second round.

'We had two fences down in the first round of the cup, I blame myself for that, I had the mare too fresh and the whole atmosphere excited her even more. I didn't ride her good enough but I nearly couldn't ride her she was that fresh. After the first round I worked her quite a bit and then got off her and got myself together, I got back up on her early for the second round and I had her in a much better place for the second round.'

How did he feel when he jumped a clear in the second round of the Aga Khan?

'It was class, Darragh Kenny had jumped clear just before me and when I went clear, the crowd started to feel we could really kick on. Unfortunately on the day, we didn't do enough to get a good result.'

Just two days later however, Bertram Allen would realise the dream of most top Irish riders when winning the Longines Grand Prix of Dublin.

'There were some riders who didn't jump their horses again in the Grand Prix after the Nations Cup but I had no doubt I was going to jump Molly again. It's not every year you will have a horse good enough to have a chance at winning a competition like that and Molly gets better the more you jump her, I knew she could jump it but I was never expecting to win the thing first time out.

'It was such a miserable day and I was the only Irish clear in the first round. I knew that American Kent Farrington is always very fast. I had jumped Molly in a speed class in Dublin the year before and I think that stood to her, it was an incredible feeling to win and I will never forget it.'

No sooner had he finished at the RDS when Bertram's focus turned to the World Equestrian Games, as following his superb run of results Robert Splaine selected the teenager as part of the Irish team for the Normandy showpiece.

Despite narrowly missing out on Olympic qualification, the Irish team produced a very solid display, with Bertram Allen finishing best of the Irish, remarkably taking seventh place in the individual standings after a week of fierce competition.

'We had a really sound bunch of lads on the team and we got on well together. It was fantastic to win the first speed competition, I thought the time would be beaten but thankfully I held on.

'We felt a bit robbed that we didn't qualify for the Olympics in Rio, one fence less down and we would have made it. We on the team are all very competitive people and the night that the team competition finished, we were all very disappointed. After the individual final we were the only country with three riders in the top 12 so it was really bad luck not to qualify. We stayed around to watch the final four, normally when you are finished jumping at a show you would be mad to get home but it's not every day you get to watch a World Championship final and the Dutch riders were just on fire and they continued that at the Furusiyya final in Barcelona, they have the best of horses, riders and management.'

Shortly after WEG Allen became the first rider to win the gold medal two years in a row with the same horse at the World Championships for Young Horses in Lanaken.

'The way it has worked out for the past few years at Lanaken has been incredible, Barnike is so competitive, to win both years with over 200 horses at the start of each week is amazing. She has been sold now to a German girl who is training with Carl Hanley and I think she is taking her to the Sunshine Tour in the spring.'

Soon afterwards, Bertram went on to take the Longines FEI World Cup Jumping series by storm, winning the five-star Italian round of the competition at Verona where, once again, he left a trail of the world's top riders in his wake.

'I had given Molly a break after the World Championships and just did one show in Liege when I brought her back. I jumped her the first day in Verona and she didn't jump that well at all and had two fences down and I was a bit worried to be honest. But Marcus (Ehning) said not to worry, that she would be perfect for the World Cup on Sunday, so we rested her on Saturday and the next day she was back to her best and felt much more relaxed with jumping indoors again.

'There are six or seven of the World Cup shows on the circuit that are extra special such as Olympia, Stuttgart and Gothenburg. Verona is one of those special shows too, it was really incredible to win. I finished the year off at Olympia and that too was special, the place was sold out every day and it's a show I would have grown up watching on TV.'

Allen recorded the fastest time of the jump-off in the World Cup at Olympia with one fence down costing him victory.

'It was the second last fence that fell, I was a bit fast to the fence before it but that's the way I ride, I always take a few chances and that's the way I will continue to ride.'

While Molly Malone, Romonov and Barnike grabbed most of the headlines during the year, the 12-year-old Montreaux mare Wild Thing L, also enjoyed another fine season and she holds a special place in Bertram's heart.

'She might not be the most talented horse in the world but she is so careful and has an incredible heart and will to win, I always believe with her if she can jump it, she can win it. My younger brother Harry jumped her in the Children on Horses during 2014 and she went well for him, she was my first junior horse so I owe her a lot of credit.

'Harry is mad keen but time will tell, he is still very young at only 13 so when he finishes ponies and does a bit of school, he will see if he still wants to go at the horses full time or not.'

Bertram first moved abroad to a yard in Germany, formerly owned by fellow Irish rider Jessica Kurten.

'I was 16 when I went to Germany on my own. I had accepted that if I wanted to get to where I needed to be, that I needed to move abroad. It was very difficult for the first six or eight months but now it is grand and we have plenty of Irish lads around. My sister April was out in Germany with me for all of 2013 and now she is back in Dublin studying in college and comes out to me every second or third weekend, she is a great help along with Mum and Dad. Alex Duffy too is a big part of the team, he has done about six or eight shows since he came here and I think he has won a class at each show. Marline, our groom, has been with me since I came to Germany and she is a great help, she drives the truck and rides out a bit as well and she lives only about 20 minutes from our stables so it's perfect.'

Having been trained in the early part of his career by Con Power, Bertram now also spends time training with former world number one, Germany's Marcus Ehning.

'I have a good relationship with Marcus, now I probably go over to him about six or eight times a year but if I have any problems, I would just send him a text or give him a ring so he is a great help. It works really well, he is a good friend.'

Bertram Allen recently picked up the prestigious Irish Independent Young Sports Star Award and he was keen to pay tribute to everyone who voted for him,

'It was very humbling so see the push that people made at home with the voting and it is something I am really thankful for, it was really nice for show jumping to win an award against major sports like football, hurling and rugby.'

Looking ahead to 2015, Bertram remains very much focused on helping the Irish team achieve their main goals for the year ahead.

'Because we were the last team that qualified for the 2015 Nations Cup series, we had the last pick as to which shows we will jump at for points this year. The Dutch got first pick as champions and I think that is only right. We have Lummen, La Baule, St Gallen and Dublin to jump at for points so we just need to get stuck in and hope to make the final in Barcelona this year.

'Early this year, I will stay with the World Cup shows and try to get enough points to qualify for the final in Las Vegas (in April) which would be very special but the big aim for this year will be the European Championships in Aachen where we hope to get one of the remaining places for the Olympics. Molly Malone is just 11 now, so she would be at a perfect age to jump in Brazil, but it will be really tough to qualify.'

Does he plan to take in some Global Champions Tour events during 2015?

'It would be nice to jump at some of those, they are incredible shows with huge prize money and my world ranking will help me get into them but for now, the Irish team is my main priority.'

Just last week, the latest World Jumping rankings saw Bertram Allen continue his rise and incredibly he is now No 15 in the world.

Could the young Irishman break into the top 10 world rankings?

'It would be great to get into the top 10 but it will be difficult, you need a big string of horses to keep collecting points and if you push too much with the same horses chasing points, their performance will suffer. I have never gone to a show or jumped in a class with just the world ranking points in mind, if you are jumping well and winning, the points will follow.'

Since that article was written, Bertram has not only made it into the top ten riders in the world, but as I write he stands at number five; Scott Brash of Great Britain is in top place.

It may seem like a meteoric rise to the top for one so young, but we have seen in the above article that it began for Bertram as a young child from the family home in Wexford, with consistent successes on ponies.

So, in April 2015 it was time for Bertram Allen and Molly Malone to travel to Las Vegas (and *en route* he won the feature five-star class in Paris with Romonov). Before this World Cup Final, the closest Ireland had ever come to taking the crown were runner-up places from Trevor Coyle and Cruising in 1999 and Jessica Kurten with Castle Forbes Libertina in 2006, while Eddie Macken and Carrolls of Dundalk were placed third in 1979. The result was a tantalisingly close third place for Allen.

Chairman of Horse Sport Ireland, Professor Pat Wall, told *The Irish Field:*

Bertram Allen is a phenomenal athlete and should really be a household name in Ireland. He does not get the due recognition that he deserves. To be fifth in the world in any sport is a phenomenal achievement. However, he does not get due recognition from the non-horsey Irish public.

He's up there with Rory McIlroy and to have achieved what he has at such a young age is just fantastic. It is only a matter of time before he is world number one in show jumping. Bertram is a great role model for our young athletes and for other riders also, regardless of age. Heartfelt congratulations to him and his family.

I have absolutely no doubt he will be world number one in the future and will win the World Cup as well. This has been a fantastic achievement for a young man – only 19 – to make it to the top five in the world show jumping rankings. He has got all it takes as a show jumping rider – brains, talents, achievement – he is the real AP McCoy of show jumping.

CAROLINE BRADLEY

The show-jumping world was shocked to the core in June 1983 when the world's leading lady rider, Caroline Bradley, collapsed at Suffolk Show and died, aged just 37.

Ronnie Massarella, British team manager, said at the time, 'I just can't grasp it. She was a tremendous girl, the greatest lady rider the world has ever seen, and a tremendous team member.

'Wherever we went people loved her.'

Caroline made her debut on the British team in 1966 when she was just 20 years old. In 1973 she took the silver medal on True Lass at the Ladies European Championships in Vienna, and a year later became the first woman to win the Puissance at the Horse of the Year Show in London. In 1975 she won the Hamburg Derby on New Yorker, becoming only the second woman to do so.

In 1978 Caroline won the Queen Elizabeth II Cup at the Royal International Horse Show on Marius; it was also a great year for her with Tigre. On him she won the team gold medal in the World Championships in Aachen, the Nice Grand Prix and the Grand Prix in Calgary.

In 1979 Caroline was again a member of the gold-medal winning British team, riding Tigre at the European Championships in Rotterdam; further wins for the pair came in the President's Cup in Calgary and the Grand Prix in Paris.

The following year she was elected Sportswoman of the Year and also appointed an MBE by the Queen. Caroline also topped the money-winners' list, won the Grand Prix at Hickstead and again won the Queen Elizabeth II Cup, this time on Tigre.

SCOTT BRASH

The man who, as I write, is number one in the world is Britain's Scott Brash, a Scotsman now based in West Sussex. The youngest of the British quartet to clinch gold in the unforgettable 2012 Olympic Games in London, Scott Brash had only been the rider of his medal-winning partner Hello Sanctos for a few months. Before that season, Brash had tried out the horse in Ukraine for show-jumping philanthropists, the carpet magnate Lord Harris of Peckham whose show-jumping involvement goes right back to Philco and David Broome in the 1970s, and DFS furniture baron Lord Kirkham. Scott Brash recommended the purchase (for a reputed £2 million) to become part of the two men's string of show jumpers, currently Hello Sailor, Hello Unique, Hello

Boyo, and Hello Annie as well as Hello Sanctos, who runs under the names of the two knights' wives, both called Pauline.

It was one of those bold moves that fully paid off. As early as March 2012 Scott Brash and Hello Sanctos had won the World Cup Grand Prix in Florida, earning $60,000. After this, Scott was given a place in the British Nations Cup team that finished sixth in Rome in May, and from there a place in the Olympic squad.

Scott Brash, born in December 1985, started riding at the age of seven on his own pony and became an enthusiastic Pony Club show jumper as a member of the Peebles Tweedale branch. He won the Scottish Indoor JA Championship with a pony called Woodlands Grasshopper.

By the age of 15, he was competing on his father's horse Intertoy Z, a Zangersheide (Belgium) Warmblood, and he proved a consistent and continuing foundation to his adult career. He also won the Foxhunter Championships for novice horses with Sauron ML, a chestnut, and was part of the British team that lifted the Aga Khan Cup in Dublin in 2011.

Both Scott Brash and Hello Sanctos have continued their winning ways since the 2012 Olympic Games in London. In 2013, they won team gold and individual bronze in the European Championships in Herning, Denmark, along with Michael Whitaker, William Funnell and fellow Olympian Ben Maher (who won the silver medal), beating eighteen other teams. In the tightest of finishes, they scored a team total of 12.18 penalties, to Germany's 12.77.

In November 2013, Scott Brash won the Doha Grand Prix on his twenty-eighth birthday, and this win gave him the overall title for the 2013 Global Champions Tour: he was the youngest rider to win it. His star continued to shine in 2014 when he won the Global Champions Tour again, and took bronze in the World Championships at Lyon. He led the world rankings for twelve successive months, the first rider to do so since German Marcus Ehning in 2006.

DAVID BROOME

Not only was David Broome one of the world's finest show jumpers but he was also, and still is, a highly respected ambassador and administrator for the sport.

He remains an icon of British show jumping, one of those names who always seems to have been there, upholding the honour of Queen and country. I had the privilege of meeting David Broome in his lovely home near Chepstow to write an article about him for a magazine in the 1990s.

HORSE HUMOUR

The boss of the Findus has made a statement saying 'horse and cow are a very similar beast'.

He's clearly never tried to win a show-jumping contest on a cow.

(Courtesy of Sickipediaorg)

It was here, at Mount Ballon Manor, Crick, near Chepstow that David Broome was born in 1940, the eldest of four children of Fred and Millie, and he has lived there ever since. One sister, Mary, was his background support and schooling rider, and the other, Liz, married Ted Edgar and she was also a top show jumper. David himself married a Liz, sister to another leading show jumper, Graham Fletcher, and they have three sons.

Mount Ballon, now preceded by the name 'The David Broome Event Centre', is home to the Wales and West Showground and much more besides, including the appropriately named café Broomies, accommodation for families as well as horses, many shows and lessons as well as livery.

One fall too many as a young child put David off riding, but luckily not for too long and at just 19 years of age he was leading money-winner with Wildfire, which Fred, his father, bought for him for less than £100. Within a year, David had won an Olympic bronze medal in Rome, in 1960, on the great Sunsalve, a character in his own right, and had become, in the process, the first British rider ever to win an Olympic show-jumping individual medal. Brothers Raimondo and Piero D'Inzeo took gold and silver on their home patch. That same year, at 20 years old, David was voted BBC Sports Personality of the Year.

With Sunsalve David also won the first of six King George V Gold Cups, still a record, and making that achievement all the more remarkable is that he won with six different horses between 1960 and 1991.

His three European Championships came with Sunsalve and twice with Mister Softee, with whom he also won an Olympic bronze medal in Mexico (1972), and one of his King George V Gold Cups.

Add to that winning the British National Championship six times, and gold in the World Championships of both La Baule in 1970 (on Beethoven) and Aachen 1978 (with Philco), along with bronzes in 1982, Dublin, on Mr Ross and 1990, Stockholm, on Lannegan.

David has been on the executive committee of the British Showjumping Association for 45 years; he was chairman in 1996–97 and has been president since 2013. It is no surprise that he was awarded OBE in 1970 and CBE in 1995. He was also Master of the Curre Hunt for many years from 1973.

On a website called 'Canter Banter', David says, 'The sport has given me so much. Being myself – that's how I see my role as President and Ambassador. I think one of my major achievements is to have served for 45 uninterrupted years on the Executive Board and that's a lot of days given to the sport.'

David has been committed to show jumping since his pony years. 'I'm still as passionate about the sport as I've always been and I love watching good jumping all day, especially young riders and horses, who are the future of our sport.'

David has also long been devoted to nurturing talent from grassroots to international level, and his dedication to developing future talents is evident at the Wales & West Showground.

'Horses are wonderful creatures and we offer everyone the chance to experience everything equestrian at our centre. I believe if you get people dipping their toes into owning a horse, they can consider which way they want to go and hopefully it's into our sport. We pride ourselves on offering a stepping stone to British Showjumping.'

Perhaps David's greatest achievement was to help steer the British team towards a famous victory in the 2012 Olympic Games in London. There can hardly have been a dry eye in the house as the Gold Medals were hung around the necks of Nick Skelton, Ben Maher, Scott Brash and Peter Charles (who had formerly represented Ireland).

It was the first time since Helsinki in 1952 that Great Britain had won team gold, with the team of Wilfred White (Nizefela), Douglas Stewart (Aherlow) and Harry Llewellyn (Foxhunter).

IRIS KELLET

Ireland's first female international civilian show jumper (followed a few years later by Diana Conolly-Carew), Iris Kellet is also remembered for her riding school on Mespil Road, Dublin which she ran almost single-handedly from a teenager following the death of her mother, Dora, and ill-health of her father, Harry.

Iris's first appearance in equestrian competition was at the age of 9, when she won Best Girl Rider at the 1935 Dublin Horse Show. Iris and her great horse Rusty competed as members of the first Irish all-civilian Nations Cup team in 1947, and won the Princess Elizabeth Cup for the European Ladies Championship at White City in 1949. The pair won it again in 1951, but a bad fall the next year resulted in a shattered ankle and a bout of tetanus, putting Iris out of top-class action for about two years.

She competed again for the Irish team in the Nations Cup during the 1960s and in 1969 she crowned her international show-jumping career by winning the European Championships in Dublin with Morning Light. Later that year Iris retired from international competition to devote herself to teaching, training and breeding horses.

In 1972 she sold the riding school on Mespil Road and moved to Kill in County Kildare. Here pupils came from many countries, and Iris trained some of the greatest names in Irish show-jumping, including Eddie Macken, Paul Darragh and Jack Doyle. She was also sought after for judging and lecturing.

As Margie McLoone said in *The Irish Times* following the death of Iris Kellet in March 2011, 'Her influence upon equestrianism in Ireland in particular, and the Irish horse industry in general, extends far beyond the medals and prizes of her competitive years.

'She set unique standards and provided inspiration for generations of Irish riders, some of whom went on from her tutelage to blaze glory across the international stage.

'... She also judged, lectured and demonstrated her skills in many countries, where her expertise in horse breeding, production, training and competition had become almost legendary.'

Many would also concur with Rory Egan's view that she was one of the greatest equestrians Ireland has ever seen and one of the most influential and respected people in Irish show jumping.

Writing in the *Sunday Independent*, Rory Egan said:

Apart from her unique horse-riding ability, Iris combined three major talents so rare in one person: a deep understanding and knowledge of horses; an ability to teach; and a shrewd business brain.

... Though strict when it came to the high standards which she demanded, she was particularly kind to young riders in her school, often walking courses with them to help them see potential problems.

... Iris Kellett's passing will merely have confirmed her place as a legend of Irish equestrianism. Her legacy is the philosophy of respect for horses that many people in the sport have carried on to this day and enhanced this country's reputation in the international horse world.

EDDIE MACKEN AND BOOMERANG

Boomerang was a chance ride for Irish rider Eddie Macken. As a young horse, Boomerang had entered his life briefly in Ireland, but the horse had then been with Ted and Liz Edgar, and was then sold to Paul Schockemöhle in Germany.

Eddie Macken had been a pupil with Ireland's famous Iris Kellet, but moved to Paul Schockemöhle's to gain more experience. Paul Schockemöhle was a star; at that stage, Boomerang was not.

Eddie Macken's father, Jimmy, a horseman himself, was a second-generation butcher in Granard, County Longford, but he realised that his son was not going to follow him into the business. From a young age all Eddie could think about was ponies and jumping, and soon the young man was being spotted at local and county shows; he had a way with horses and it was clear that, given the right chances, he had the talent to go to the top. Before long, he joined Iris Kellet as a working pupil.

While he was there, one of the young horses to come in was called Battle Boy; bred in County Tipperary by Jimmy Murphy, the youngster was by the thoroughbred Battleburn out of the Murphy's Irish draft mare, Girl From The Brown Mountain. The Murphys educated him in the Kilmogany Harriers hunting field and on the local show-jumping circuit, before sending him to 'finishing school' at Kellet's. After a couple of years there, he was sold to Ted Edgar for his wife, Liz, sister of David Broome, to ride. In 1975, by now 9 years old, he was sold on to Dr Herbert Schnapka, an owner in Paul and Alwin Schockemöhle's Muhlen yard, south-west of Stuttgart – and renamed Boomerang.

By this time, Eddie had also moved to that yard in order to widen his European experience. One day in 1975, his best horse died in a freak accident and Schockemöhle is famously said to have told him, 'take my speed horse Boomerang for the time being, until you get something better.'

At the time, Boomerang was 'mouthy' and so he came to be ridden in a hackamore, which is a bridle without a bit, operated by exerting pressure on the horse's nose via metal strips each side of the noseband.

Eddie Macken and Boomerang became household names; they went on to win a record four Hickstead Derbies from 1976 to 1979 and the 1976 Hamburg Derby, and they were in the winning Aga Khan team for Ireland for three successive years, from 1977 to 1979, along with Paul Darragh, Con Power and James Kernan. In 1977, Dr Schnapka gave Boomerang to Macken.

They won or were placed second in thirty-two European and American Grand Prix and Derby events – and they missed out on the World Championships by one quarter of a time fault. This was in Aachen in 1978; Boomerang went clear for all four finalist riders in the last change-horse round but when Eddie Macken was riding Pandur Z he made a miscalculation and picked up a quarter of a time fault and the slip cost him the gold.

'Boomerang deserved to be world champion,' Macken told the Press afterwards. 'Well, he was world champion because he was the best horse there. I wasn't. I was the one who made the mistake.'

When he and Boomerang were at their peak, Macken was barred from competing at the Olympic Games because he was a professional and had sponsorship (Boomerang had been renamed Carroll's Boomerang).

In his last season, Boomerang remained at the top of the show-jumping tree. He paid his first visit to Calgary, Canada in September and won the main class every day, including the Grand Prix. The next month they won their fourth (and final) Horse of the Year Show Grand Prix at Wembley, followed by two wins in the Dublin Indoor International in November. A fourth at Olympia before Christmas was to bring the curtain down on Boomerang's illustrious international career.

Boomerang retired in 1980 and was put down three years later; he is buried in Rafaheen Stud, Kells, County Meath, now home to Macken's first wife, Suzie (Macken moved to Canada and is remarried). Boomerang's grave is surrounded by four evergreens, symbolising his record of four consecutive Hickstead Derby wins, four Wembley championships, four clear rounds in the 1978 World Championship final, and four years in a row without knocking a fence at the Aga Khan Trophy in Dublin.

Eddie Macken is something of an evergreen himself. In 1998 he took part in his twenty-seventh consecutive Aga Khan, and ten years later, in July 2008, the 59-year-old returned to Hickstead for the first time in a decade. The following month, at Dublin Show, the Irish cheered him home as he represented his country once more and jumped clear in a flawless second round to help clinch second place in the Aga Khan.

BEN MAHER

Ben Maher and Scott Brash represented youth in Great Britain's Olympic gold-medal winning team in London 2012. Nick Skelton and Peter Charles were the mature members and, perhaps one could say, recovered crocks: apart from a serious neck injury, Skelton also sported a replacement hip and had had both shoulder and knee surgery, while Charles had previously broken his spine.

Ben Maher was no stranger to riding at the highest level; he had already competed at an Olympic Games, in Beijing 2008, at the age of 25 and participated in the 2009 European Championships, and a year before the Olympics he had won a bronze medal in the European Championships in Madrid. He had also won the 2005 Hickstead Derby on Alfredo II and the 2010 Puissance at Olympia on Noctambule Courcelle. A year later, at the pre-Christmas London show, he won the World Cup qualifying class on his home-bred Tripple XIII

Born in Enfield, Greater London, Ben Maher already had his sights set on show jumping when he left school. He trained initially with Liz Edgar in Warwickshire before moving to Switzerland under the tutelage of world-star rider Beat Mandli (whose sister-in-law, Lesley McNaught, was a talented British show jumper).

DID YOU KNOW?

Larry Kiely of Ireland jointly held the World Puissance Record at 7ft 2in at one time; he also competed in the 1968 Mexico Olympics.

Look at photos of Boomerang, Eddie Macken's record-breaking show jumper, and you will see he wore a hackamore, that is, a bitless bridle. At an English show one year a child was heard to say of another horse, 'Oh look, he's wearing a Boomerang!

ALAN OLIVER

Alan Oliver and Red Admiral were my childhood show-jumping heroes, and in later years I often saw Alan as he became a sought-after course designer.

He died in September 2006, and a leading show-jumping correspondent Genevieve Murphy paid tribute to him in *The Times*, which is reproduced here, courtesy of *The Times*.

Alan Arthur Jack Oliver, show-jumping rider and course designer: born Kimble Wick, Buckinghamshire 8 September 1932; married 1954 Gene Whewell (marriage dissolved), 1964 Alison Coulton (marriage dissolved); died Dunstable, Bedfordshire 10 September 2006.

Alan Oliver was a beanpole lad of 11 when he first emerged on the adult show-jumping scene riding his father's horses and a hunter on loan from a garage owner, Harry Payne. Both his size and his acrobatic style would have made him easily recognisable – and so would the number of prizes won by the young farmer's son.

By his late teens and early twenties Oliver, had a wonderful string of horses to ride. He partnered six of them – Red Admiral, Red Star, Galway Boy, Sheila, John Gilpin and Planet – in the 1953 Leading Show Jumper of the Year at Harringay, where he achieved a phenomenal result by filling six of the top seven places. 'I just kept jumping them off one after the other,' he said, 'I won it with Red Admiral and when we walked into the ring and I looked up at the board I thought: "That's funny – there's nobody else up there."'

Red Admiral, probably the best horse he ever rode, was also his mount in a memorable duel with the German Olympic captain, Fritz Thiedemann, in the 1954 King George V Gold Cup at White City. Time had not yet been introduced as the deciding factor in a jump-off, so the two riders completed five rounds in an atmosphere of mounting tension before Thiedemann prevailed on Meteor.

By the time David Broome appeared on the adult scene in the mid-1950s, Oliver (though only 7 years older) was already an old hand. According to Broome he was also the friendliest rider of all:

'There was never anything aloof about him; he was always prepared to speak to up-and-coming riders and give them encouragement.'

Oliver became known to a wider radio audience in 1957 after he 'sold' a horse called Red Link to *The Archers*. The producer's idea was to 'buy' a novice horse early in the year and follow its progress through to victory in the Foxhunter Championship at the Horse of the Year Show in October. Oliver did point out that picking just one horse to win at Harringay was about a 10,000-to-one shot, but they still went ahead.

Having become part of the continuing story of Ambridge, he was rather embarrassed when *The Archers* visited show after show at which Red Link failed to jump a single clear round. Eventually, however, he did win a Foxhunter class and he was third in a regional final, which qualified him for Harringay. The cliffhanger ended with Red Link finishing second in the final, which, considering the odds, was a tremendous achievement.

Oliver was a strong contender for an Olympic place in 1952 and 1956, but he was not selected on either occasion – partly, one assumes, because most of his victories were then gained on the home circuit where courses were less sophisticated than abroad. He was to go through a lean period as his great string of horses eventually came to the end of their careers, but he never thought of giving up. 'I was always under the impression that, however good you are or whatever horses your ride, you're only a champion for that one day – in this job you're a 24-hour champion,' he said.

Though he maintained his slim figure, he did adapt his style before more good horses (including Pitz Palu and Sweep, who was his mount on winning Nations Cup teams at Barcelona in 1969 and London in 1972) arrived at his yard. Courses had become longer and more technical, so it was important to stay closer to the saddle. He believed that his rides in steeplechases and point-to-points had helped him 'because it taught me to sit on them'.

He had begun course designing before he retired from competition and was therefore able to remain a convivial presence on the show-jumping scene. Among many others, he designed courses for the World Cup final in Gothenburg, shows in Toronto, New York, Sydney and Melbourne plus most of the county shows in Britain.

NICK SKELTON

Nick Skelton began riding almost before he could walk, but as a teenager the lad who was to become a world-class show jumper wanted to be a National Hunt jockey, and would gallop his show-jumping pony round and round the field, riding with short stirrups pretending to be a jockey. But one day, at 14 years old, he took his pony over to Ted and Liz Edgar for some schooling and the rest, as they say, is history.

In 1974 and 1975 he took two team silvers and an individual gold at the Junior European Championships. As a fully fledged adult he competed many times at the European Show Jumping Championships, winning three golds, three silvers and three bronzes both individually and with the British team over several decades.

A highlight of Nick's career came back in 1978 when he broke the British equestrian high-jump record, clearing over 7ft 7in on Lastic in London. In the Olympic Games he won a silver in the 'alternative' games in Rotterdam and most recently in London 2012 he won a Team Gold Medal.

In 2000 Nick's life was in danger for some days after he broke his neck in a show-jumping fall in Cheshire. As he slowly recovered, it was thought he would never ride again, let alone compete. Up until that time he had already broken the world record for Nations Cup team appearances (122) and had 137 Great Britain 'caps' to his credit (including Olympic Games, World and European Championships). He won the Hickstead Derby three times, the King George V Gold Cup four times and the World Cup once. He also won fifty-eight International Grand Prix competitions.

Yet one year after that life-threatening injury he was back in the saddle, and recommenced competing in 2002. In 2004 Nick looked like he was going to gain the Olympic medal that had so far eluded him; he was leading in Athens until the last round on Arco, owned by John Hales who is also a leading National Hunt owner, and was president of the British Showjumping Association from 2005 to 2008. However, three fences down on the second day dropped him out of the medals. Nick Skelton's turn was finally to come eight years after Athens when he won that memorable Olympic Gold Medal in London 2012, at the age of 55.

Perhaps reflecting Nick's early ambition to race-ride, today both his sons are fully immersed in National Hunt racing. Dan is a successful trainer from beside his father's show-jumping stables in Warwickshire, and Harry, who is the youngest rider ever to win the Irish Grand National, is his stable jockey.

Nick Skelton is one of Britian's most successful international riders and his medal haul is formidable:

Year	Competition	Location	Event	Medal
1974	Junior European Championships	Lucerne	Team Jumping	Silver
1975	Junior European Championships	Dornbirn	Team Jumping	Silver
1975	Junior European Championships	Dornbirn	Individual Jumping	Gold
1980	Alternative Olympics	Rotterdam	Team Jumping	Silver
1985	European Championships	Dinard	Team Jumping	Gold
1982	World Championships	Dublin	Team Jumping	Bronze
1986	World Championships	Aachen	Team Jumping	Silver
1986	World Championships	Aachen	Individual Jumping	Bronze
1987	European Championships	St Gallen	Team Jumping	Gold
1987	European Championships	St Gallen	Individual Jumping	Bronze
1989	European Championships	Rotterdam	Team Jumping	Gold
1990	World Championships	Stockholm	Team Jumping	Bronze
1991	European Championships	La Baule	Team Jumping	Silver
1993	European Championships	Gijon	Team Jumping	Silver
1995	European Championships	St Gallen	Team Jumping	Silver
1998	World Championships	Rome	Team Jumping	Bronze
2011	European Championships	Madrid	Team Jumping	Bronze
2011	European Championships	Madrid	Individual Jumping	Bronze
2012	Olympic Games	London	Team Jumping	Gold

HARVEY SMITH

Beneath Harvey Smith's blunt, broad Yorkshire image lies a master of his chosen art of show jumping. Yes, he could be controversial but on a horse he was sublime; no one was better at seeing a stride and 'lifting' a horse over a fence. The crowds loved him.

The crowds came to his rescue in 1971 after his infamous 'V sign' gesture when he won the Hickstead Derby for the second successive year. Harvey Smith was stripped of his £2,000 prize money, but huge publicity and public backing saw him reinstated. He was later to admit in interviews that he was indeed making an obscene sign.

A Yorkshire builder's son, Harvey was a self-taught rider and he seldom, if ever, bought either ready-made or expensive horses; instead, he had an eye for a young horse, and the ability to bring the best out in it.

Like other top riders of his generation (he was born in 1938), he missed out on Olympic selection during the short-lived era when professional riders were not eligible, but he rode in them twice before then, in Mexico City 1968 and in Munich 1972, where he finished fourth in the individual competition. The championships where he excelled were the European Championships, in which he became almost a standing dish. He participated five times and on all five occasions he brought home a medal; he also won a record-equalling four Hickstead Derbies.

Harvey Smith retired from show jumping in 1990, the year that his wife, Sue (*née* Maslen) took out a racehorse trainer's licence.

Today, Harvey Smith can occasionally be seen giving interviews at usually northern race meetings after a win by one of the horses trained by Sue from their place on top of the rugged Yorkshire moors. He sounds much like he always did.

In 2013 Sue Smith trained Aurora's Encore to win the Grand National at Aintree at odds of 66 to 1, which prompted an insightful article by Ian Chadband in the *Daily Telegraph* shortly before the 2014 Grand National. It was with some difficulty that he persuaded Harvey to speak with him. At length, he succeeded and unearthed some nuggets:

'Talk to her [Sue]. What the hell do you wanna talk to me for? Sixty years I've had of this. That's why I dodge to the back, I'm always trying to lose identity, not gain it,' he roars, before eventually softening and agreeing to talk after the next race from Towcester.

Dear Harvey. At 75, he is just as you would hope he might be, as legend always had it; one minute, curmudgeonly, difficult, blunt and as stubborn as 'owt that ever drew breath in God's Own County.

Then the next opinionated, fun and as entertaining as he was in his seventies heyday when his was one of the most famous faces in the land and his V-sign gesture to the Hickstead judges made a nation either titter or tut.

There is no stopping him. On the demise of show jumping as one of Britain's favourite TV sports?

'The BBC ruined it by not showing it live, editing it and losing all the drama.'

'A lot of people the BHA [British Horseracing Authority] employ don't understand National Hunt racing like we do.'

'We've always been everyday people, not your flash in the pan. My skill is spotting young horses and buying the raw material.'

'We make silk purses out of sow's ears. All on sensible money, not ridiculous money.'

On the success of their training operation here at Craiglands Farm, where they have prepared close to 1,000 winners?

'We just buy a nice young 'un and bring him on. We don't have to go and pay millions for the horses like all these southern lot are doing.'

On how life has changed since last year's National win with Auroras Encore?

'It hasn't. We've been getting horses prepared for ever. They say: "How long did you celebrate?" We didn't. No fuss; this was just another day in life for us.'

And on the partnership between him and Sue?

'I think we are one of the best teams in horse racing, definitely.'

PAT SMYTHE

Pat Smythe, born in 1928, was the first big female show-jumping star and holds a special place in show-jumping history. She had two older brothers, one of whom died from pneumonia aged four, and when Pat was the same age she nearly died from diphtheria, and had to learn to walk again. She grew up in Richmond Park but was evacuated to the Cotswolds during the Second World War with her pony, and that area became her home until she moved to Switzerland after she married.

Pat's parents managed to get out of France under gunfire on the last boat from Bordeaux just before the town, and most of France, was occupied by the Germans. They both died when Pat was a young adult. It was while in the Cotswolds that Pat began jumping at local shows and gymkhanas and then took part in an international show with a mare called Finality (whose dam was said to have pulled a milk cart), doing so well that in 1947 she was selected for the British team, along with Harry Llewellyn, Ruby Holland-Martin, Tony Robeson and Brian Butler. Finality was sold by its owner, and another good mare, Leona, had to be sold after Pat's mother died.

It was then that she bought her cheapest horse, the ex-racehorse Prince Hal for £150. He arrived as a poor-tempered, one-sided hot chestnut. He was followed for the same price by the mare Tosca who, after an unpromising start, sealed Pat's route to stardom. At first, Tosca was wild and had a dislike of human beings, but worse, the first time she jumped a Cotswold stone wall near home she ran away with Pat for three circuits of the field before Pat could pull her up – and then the mare started fly-bucking. She then refused to jump the next stone wall. Months of patient flat work followed to produce the show jumper that is still remembered today.

On her first overseas trip with the British team in 1947, Pat was the only member of the team to jump a clear round in the Grand Prix at Brussels. She was named Show Jumper of the Year at the first Horse of the Year Show, aged 21. That year Pat returned to Brussels to take the Grand Prix on Nobbler. It is said that the D'Inzeo brothers of Italy and Paco Goyoaga of Spain searched the rule book, looking for a hidden clause that would eliminate Pat for being female.

When Pat had begun competing, women were ineligible for the Nations Cup, Olympic show jumping and three-day event disciplines. She won the 1956 Grand Prix Militaire in Lucerne, but she and the lady rider who had finished second had to cede the trophy to the French officer who came third.

Pat was a woman in a man's world and it was certainly tough for her, financially too, but she supplemented her income by writing successful children's pony books.

In her *Pat Smythe's Book of Horses* (Cassell and Company, 1955) she recalls some of those early forays abroad and the different types of courses they found; it was before uniformity in either types of fence or even scoring, and horses were often stabled a few miles away.

She wrote, 'Since the last war, the standard of national show jumping has improved out of all recognition, due to the greater emphasis placed upon international competition and to the increased share taken by civilian riders in the sport.'

Not all international shows had kept pace, but White City in London 'has become recognised throughout the world as the best, both from the point of view of the courses and the excellent organization.'

In Madrid, the fences were big with wide spreads and the classes were judged on speed. Grooms had to hack the horses to the venue and hang around in the blazing sun. It was also probably the first show that allowed betting.

In Lisbon, a long-striding or bold horse was needed to cope with the length between fences. Prince Hal won a six-bar competition in which the last three fences stood at over 6ft with about 12 yards in between each. At least the horses had stables beside the showground there, and plenty of shade. The riders were also plied with vintage wine by the venue owner, and the jumping itself took place in the centre of the racecourse.

Pat found the outdoor arena in Rome one of the most beautiful in the world, at the Piazza di Siena in the Borghesi Gardens. The poles there were light, and knocked down easily, and the fences were colourful but set at awkward distances; 'however,' she wrote, 'this made for a high standard of jumping so the only solution is to practise more at home over varying distances between fences and over water jumps so that we can overcome the problem.'

The dominant Italian riders at the time were the D'Inzeo brothers, Raimondo and Piero, and they remained so for a number of decades.

In North Africa, at Algiers, the show was held inside the racecourse, but on sand, making for deep going for the course over big, solid fences.

The whole show was looked upon as an elaborate party by the organisers, and we thoroughly enjoyed their hospitality. We were taken to the President's house about a hundred miles inland, through breath-taking countryside of lovely hills and orange groves. It was an extraordinary sensation to realize that within an hour's drive from Algiers one could go skiing, have a swim in the sea, or ride a camel in the desert.

Pat found her first experience of Dublin 'unique'. 'The Dublin arena is magnificent and I got a great thrill riding over the permanent course with the double and single banks, the stone wall and deep water jump.'

Of mixing the hectic social scene with the business of show jumping when abroad, she admitted it wasn't always easy. 'When we are competing at official shows we are usually invited for drinks to each of the embassies in the capital, and since these parties nearly always take place just before the shows, it is difficult to do full justice to the generous hospitality.'

At home Pat found Harringay in London one of the great indoor shows of the world, but the arena was not large and there was little space for preliminary warm up. The arena in Paris was of similar size, and with even less exercise area, yet the venue could seat 15,000 people 'and the spectators are so keen that they pay up to £3 for a seat'.

Marseilles, by contrast, was much bigger both for arena and exercise. In Zurich all the international riders were put up in the same hotel, 'a most pleasing feature ... it was most refreshing to be able to meet one's rivals on a social rather than a competitive basis for a change.' The surface, however, was laid on top of an ice-rink, which occasionally caused some slippery problems.

In America Pat found the two international shows at Harrisburg, Pennsylvania, and New York, 'lagging behind their European counterparts. For one thing, with the exception of the Thousand-Dollar Stakes, there was no prize money; also, the fences were not up to European standards.'

From Harrisburg the horses were conveyed in articulated trucks, six per vehicle, and driven at speeds of 70mph to New York, where facilities for stabling and exercise proved a nightmare – but the hospitality at the Waldorf Hotel where the riders stayed was extremely generous.

Toronto in Canada, by contrast, was 'exceedingly well organised' with ample and airy stables and a small exercise arena and a large main arena, but the course design lacked ingenuity.

The logistics of travelling were considerable with every stitch of wear for both horse and rider being taken with them; not just clean breeches in Pat's case, but cocktail dresses, too. Food and fodder, grooming kit, tack and make-up all went with the groom, for whom the journey might be by road, rail or air; some of the train journeys took five hours, and Pat's groom, Pauline, would never once leave her charges' sides during all that time.

By the mid-1950s Pat Smythe was sweeping all before her, and fan mail came by the sackful; the letters sometimes included marriage proposals including one on behalf of a member of the Russian team, with promises of the best horses and training; she said she received a total of five proposals in four languages, but in the end it was her lifelong friend, Swiss three-day event rider Sam Koechlin, whom she married.

DID YOU KNOW?

At the RDS show in Dublin no lady was allowed to ride in any jumping competition until 1919. In that year a novelty class for women was introduced. From 1920 women were able to compete nationally. In 1954, thanks to an international rule, women were finally permitted to compete in the international competitions.

Traditionally, the Ladies Hunter Classes for ladies riding side-saddle at the Dublin Horse Show, wearing the veil and habit costume, were judged on the Thursday of the show. As a result Thursday became Ladies' Day.

For sixteen years, between 1947 and 1963, Pat Smythe became a household name: she was national ladies' champion eight times, and four-time European ladies' champion. She was the first woman to win a medal (bronze) in the hitherto men-only show-jumping event at the 1956 Olympic Games in Stockholm, and she won the second ever running of the Hickstead Derby. Pat died in 1996, aged 67.

4

HORSES

CRUISING

The horse-breeding world was stunned to learn in early 2015 that Cruising, the world-famous Irish show-jumping stallion, had not only been cloned, but doubly so. In a further well-kept secret at Mary McCann's Hartwell Stud in County Kildare, the two offspring were already 3 years old, and due to take up stud duties themselves later in the year.

Cruising was not only one of Ireland's top show jumpers, but he also sired top show jumpers and eventers. Ridden by Trevor Coyle, he won many Grand Prix, including in Aachen, Dortmund and Lucerne, and he was a mainstay on Irish Nations Cup teams.

Bred by Bord na gCapall (Irish Horse Board) in 1985, he was by the Irish Draught Sea Crest, also a Grade-A show jumper, out of the top international jumping mare Mullacrew (by Nordlys). She had been given to the Bord by the army, and the Bord, in turn, selected Mary McCann to have her for breeding, as part of a programme to improve Irish sport-horse breeding.

Just a month before dying in September 2014, Cruising was cheered by thousands of fans when paraded at the Dublin Horse Show, but unbeknownst to them, some of his DNA was extracted that month and inserted into empty eggs; the embryos that resulted were then implanted into surrogate mares.

Bord na gCapall was formed in 1976 specifically to promote the non-thoroughbred horse industry following many casualties in the two world wars, combined with the demise of the animals as work horses on the land as tractors took over; the Bord was disbanded in the 1980s. Nowadays, all Irish horse-breeding and sport, with the exception of racing, is under the umbrella of Horse Sport Ireland.

Cruising, Clover and King of Diamonds were the cream of a golden era of Irish show-jumping stallions; now two of one of them stand again.

GO-SLY-UP

Show jumpers come in all shapes and sizes, but at the top level the general model would be a fairly large, well-bred 'sport horse' with a bit of blood in him, and who must also be athletic. As with all 'rules', there are, of course, exceptions; of these, the pony Stroller was probably the most phenomenal; also, Ryan's Son did not 'look like a show jumper'.

Back in the mid-1950s and '60s there was a small stocky Irish cob who became such a 'standing dish' at shows the length and breadth of Ireland that spectators barely watched, knowing he would jump clear. This was a little grey horse called Go-Sly-Up ('Up Sligo' in reverse).

Go-Sly-Up began his life hauling telegraph poles during the electrification of the West of Ireland. He would be ridden home bareback and bridleless after his day's work, jumping whatever obstacles came his way, including the telegraph poles lying on the ground.

Frank McGarry, a cattle dealer and show-jumping enthusiast from Sligo, was told of him at the end of a show one day, watched him jump a line of 5ft fences with only a rope around his neck, and bought him for £75.

No one could have foreseen that this little cob would become the most successful show jumper in Irish history, and probably the world – then and now. From the start he was a gentle horse who also became a huge character at home; he was also very strong. Within a week or two of buying him, Frank McGarry took him to his first show, at Belturbet in County Cavan. There, ridden by Francie Kerins, he won the two classes he contested.

Standing just 15.1hh and with his modest breeding – by 'Nothing' out of 'Nothing' – Go-Sly-Up did not raise big expectations, yet eleven years later he had won 513 first prizes at registered shows; the previous national record was 22. This was before there were timed jump-offs, and so he might have to jump as many as six rounds until he was 'the last man standing'.

Frank says, 'He had little if any pure blood in him and other people considered him probably the plainest horse I ever owned or jumped, but there was something very likeable about him and he was a grand type of cob.'

He was by the same sire as The Brat, whose owner, Willie Hughes, said the sire had very little breeding at all. His progeny from ordinary mares were all good jumpers, so if he had been put to thoroughbred or three-quarter-bred mares the results could have been phenomenal.

'My father used to say "an ounce of breeding is worth ten tens of feeding,"' Frank recalls, yet from the first Go-Sly-Up was a star in the

HORSE HUMOUR

I went riding today.
Horseback?
Sure. It came back before I did.

making. He jumped for eleven seasons, from 1955 to 1966, and after his first season he had already reached Grade A and was mostly jumping in Grand Prix and Puissance, the highest grade of show jumping over the most challenging tracks. It was this precocity that led Frank into letting his youngster go to the RDS Dublin Show in Ballsbridge.

Go-Sly-Up was overfaced (asked to achieve more than he was physically or mentally ready for) and stopped, something that became virtually unknown in his life. Frank never returned him to Dublin and the little grey horse never looked back, bar the time he nearly died at home. Frank had bought a new horse, a bay called Westport, from Tommy Brennan's father, Mattie, in Kilkenny, after watching it at Burton Hall. He stabled it in a former cottage that Frank had converted to a double stable. (It was before he built new stables at Carrowmore, the indoor arena he established outside Sligo, now run by his son, Declan.)

Go-Sly-Up was in one side and Westport in the other. During the night they must have had a fierce fight and in the morning Go-Sly-Up was found lying motionless on the floor, covered in bites and kicks, unable to get up. In spite of regular veterinary treatment, he lay there for weeks, virtually wasting away.

One day, an English vet who was visiting suggested that the problem might be muscle damage to a shoulder and suggested operating on it. He gave a 50:50 chance of success.

It was like opening a can of worms: buckets of poison poured out of the incision and by the time the vet had finished the filthy matter had spread right across the yard. When the little horse came round it was as if relief was spread across his face. He got up, walked around, and every day brought improvement.

Only a few short weeks later Frank saddled him and rode him down to the back field; there, he popped him over a few fences, and he was fine. Frank brought him back to the stable, clipped him, and told a surprised Cecil Mahon, his groom, that he was taking him, unshod, to Boyle Show the next day.

There, Cecil won all three of his competitions; it was just as if he'd never been away.

'He was so reliable that people almost turned away when he was jumping, knowing what the result was going to be,' Frank says. 'Only once do I remember him having a fence down, and that was at a show in Inniscrone. People said, "He's finished," but I said, "not at all."'

Ballina was another local show, and Frank remembers the high-wall jumping continuing until it was nearly dark.

'But the people wouldn't go home; there were about 12,000 of them, it was their interest of the year.'

Fans of the little horse spread further afield than Ireland. There was a time when a German author by the name of Ursula knocked on Frank's door and asked if she could see Go-Sly-Up; she was writing a book and wanted to include him. She then asked if she could sit up on him, and couldn't believe her luck when permission was granted. She would not have been allowed near such a famous horse in Germany.

Ursula rode him down the road, then said she would like to take a picture of him jumping. At that moment Cecil Mahon was cycling along the road, wearing shoes and trousers, so he got up on Go-Sly-Up and jumped a wall on him.

'The girl couldn't believe her eyes,' says Frank, 'she thought I'd just got a passer-by to jump him.'

This was also the time when there was no winter show jumping, and so Go-Sly-Up was turned out on the farm, along with others, during the off season. He knew it was his holiday, and wouldn't allow himself to be caught, except by his groom Cyril Mahon, who usually carried the cob's favourite sweets in his pocket.

Cecil worked for Frank for seventeen years, and was one of his early riders, including on Go-Sly-Up. When it came to show day, Cecil would call to Go-Sly-Up saying that it was time to go and, unaided, the horse would walk out of his unlatched stable and up the ramp into the horsebox, and would put himself into whatever stall Cecil told him to.

The rider most associated with Go-Sly-Up, and who began his international career with Frank McGarry, was Francie Kerins. He started working for Frank as a schoolboy in the mid-1950s and stayed until the early 1970s. He says that during his time with Frank, and especially on the foreign tours, he made many lifelong friends. He married in 1974 after which he reduced international appearances and concentrated instead on bringing on young horses. Among his future clients was Ann Smurfit. His son, Darragh, jumped on the winning Aga Khan team in 2012.

The *Farming Independent* noted that Frank and Francie had for many years been the leading combination in national competitions and 'by their efforts did much to foster what was a dying sport in the West of Ireland'.

At Ballinasloe on the last day of the season in 1966, when Go-Sly-Up had been jumping for eleven years and was still at the top, a man stood beside Frank at the ringside without knowing he was the horse's owner. There was a particularly high fence for the Puissance, standing at about 6ft high.

'Will the little grey horse ever jump that big fence?' he mused.

'If he jumps that he'll never jump another,' Frank said.

The man, not knowing the horse, replied, 'You're right, if he jumps that, that'll finish him,' meaning he would be overfaced.

Without telling anyone in advance, least of all his rider, Frank had decided to bring the curtain down on the horse's career while he was still at the height of his prowess.

Go-Sly-Up, of course, cleared the fence in question, won the class – his 513th – and retired. He had more than earned it. Throughout his career Frank had turned down many offers, including blank cheques for Go-Sly-Up; instead he kept him as his 'shop window'. There could have been no better advertisement for his wares.

Later that year Frank McGarry, Francie Kerrins and Go-Sly-Up were honoured by the people of Sligo; they were given a presentation after they had paraded through the town.

Go-Sly-Up lived contentedly on the farm for ten years after his retirement, lapping up attention from admiring visitors.

Frank went out to him as usual one cold and frosty winter's morning, and found him lying on the ground, unable to get up because of arthritis. The horse lifted his head as Frank approached him. Frank knew what he had to do.

'He was a darling horse,' he says, his eyes filling with tears at the memory of him almost fifty years later.

MILTON

'When he takes off, you felt that you'd never come down' – so John Whitaker is quoted as saying of the white-grey Milton who became a superstar and favourite of show-jumping audiences everywhere.

Milton was by the Dutch Warmblood stallion Marius (bred by Hans Werner Ritters), and out of Aston Answer owned by John Harding-Rolls. Caroline had had much show-jumping success on Marius so was keen to buy the offspring; in 1977 she succeeded in buying the colt foal who was to turn white; naturally, it was planned that he should become her ride. Instead, when that foal was now a promising seven-year-old gelding, she died.

She was an incredibly hard grafter, and the thought was she had literally worked herself to death. For instance, Caroline was not one to expect staff to work on Christmas Day; she would make sure they enjoyed their festivities and would do the work of several people herself.

Milton was still young for a show jumper, but Caroline had already harboured high hopes of him being an Olympic horse for her. Instead, her parents, Tom and Doreen, had the harrowing task of dispersing or, in a few cases, keeping all twenty-nine of her horses. Milton was one whose ownership they retained.

DID YOU KNOW?

Britain did not excel at show jumping in the 1920s and '30s. The rules varied from event to event. The groundwork for the new British show-jumping scene had been drafted in 1942 in PoW camp Oflag IX A/H, Spannenburg, by three British officers who had represented the nation at show jumping before they went to war: Colonel Mike Ansell, Bede Cameron and Nat Kindersley. There would be greater professionalism in training and the design of courses, time limits and better fences. They got speedy results: the all-male British team took bronze at the 1948 London Olympics, despite never having been closer than seventh before.

Just fifty-six clear rounds were jumped in the first fifty-four years of the Hickstead Derby in Sussex. In some years there was no clear round, and on a few occasions there was no more than one.

In due course, after time off because of an injury incurred while clipping, Milton became John Whitaker's ride – and this was to become the most-successful-ever partnership up to that time in show jumping. They jumped seven consecutive double clears in Nations Cups, won silver and gold medals in European Championships, and were twice in the FEI World Cup Final. Not surprisingly, he was considered the mainstay for the 1988 Olympic Games in Seoul, but Caroline Bradley's parents, who still owned him, would not allow him to travel there, fearing the journey would be too much. As a result he was banned from Nations Cups teams for a season (which I would imagine would have hurt Great Britain more than the owners) – and when he retired at Olympia in 1994 it was as show jumping's first equine millionaire, having earned £1¼ million.

Milton retired to the Whitakers' Yorkshire farm and made some public appearances until he had to have major colic surgery in 1998. He survived that, but sadly within the year he suffered another bout of colic and died.

John Whitaker recalled in a *Horse and Hound* interview about the equine star, 'He often had a battle of wills with our grooms and would push them as far as he could by rooting to the spot or refusing to go into his stable. He also used to take his rugs off and shred them, and if he didn't fancy doing something, he would blow raspberries.'

Ronnie Massarella, Britain's *chef d'équipe*, was quoted as saying, 'Milton gave me my greatest years in the sport and he and John were the perfect ambassadors for British showjumping. Milton had something no other horse had.'

RYAN'S SON

It looked an innocuous enough fall, and Ryan's Son, the International star that John Whitaker had once refused to ride 'because he looked like a carthorse', walked out of the Hickstead ring apparently none the worse for his fall at some parallel poles in the Derby.

But a few hours later, the Olympic-team silver medallist collapsed and died, probably from an internal haemorrhage. It was 1987, and Ryan's Son was 18 years old.

In April 2015 John Whitaker reminisced on his great hero when he was guest editor for *Horse and Hound*. He described how he keeps a piece of mane and tail from his great horse at his Yorkshire home. He also told of how unimpressed he was when, at 17, he saw the horse for the first time and considered him 'a cart horse with big feet, big head, too much white on him, a ewe neck and standing barely 16hh.' Ryan's son had a paltry fifty points on his official card when Malcolm Barr, who was to become John's father-in-law, gave the teenager the horse.

At first, to John's surprise, he and Ryan's Son clicked and notched up a string of successes at local shows. But at the Great Yorkshire Show he was out of his depth and knocked many fences, receiving a score fellow Yorkshiremen would be proud of in cricket – but not the young man jumping at his own county show. Humiliated in front of his home crowd, he told his father, Donald, that he would not return the next day.

But return he did – and won his class, beating his childhood heroes David Broome and Harvey Smith.

'It was unbelievable,' John told *Horse and Hound*. 'I had looked up to those two all my life, particularly Harvey Smith because he was a Yorkshireman. I had tried to copy what they had done and had beaten them. Just one day changes everything in your life. From that point on, I never looked back. Ryan put me on the map, and if it were not for him, I would still be a milkman.'

During the next fourteen years, the bay gelding with the big white face always wore the same bit with which he arrived as a 4-year-old – a rusty-looking twisted snaffle with long cheek pieces, one of which was broken. He was also an endearing character; one trait that his fans adored was his habit of bucking after the last fence.

'He was showing off,' said John. 'He knew he had finished by the applause and by feeling me switch off the pressure. He said: "that's it, I have done it", and bucked. It was off-putting, though, if the audience clapped after a difficult combination in the middle of a round, because he bucked then too, which would put you wrong for the next fence.'

His greatest asset was his consistency and he was almost guaranteed to jump a clear round. From a young age Ryan was inclined to hot up, and so, on his father's advice, John used to turn him out in the field between shows – and he says Ryan was always a 'nice person'.

Together, John and Ryan travelled around the world, winning silver in the European Championships, bronze in the World Championships, the 1983 Hickstead Derby, in which they were also second three times and, finally, when Ryan was 17, the King George V Gold Cup, in addition to the 1984 Olympic silver in Los Angeles. For ten years, Ryan was the biggest money-winner on the circuit. All of this might never have been, had things gone differently when he was still a youngster.

Alan Smith, the now-retired *Daily Telegraph* correspondent, remembers:

John Whitaker and Ryan's Son might well have made their Olympic debut eight years earlier than when winning a team silver in 1984, though if they had it would probably have cost the horse his long and honourable career. All through the early part of 1976 John, with Ryan's Son, and Debbie Johnsey with Moxy were on great form, and, though the youngest of the riders in consideration – John was 20 and Debbie just 18, looked to have booked their places for Montreal when jumping clear rounds in the Swiss Nations Cup in Lucerne.

Moxy also jumped a double clear in Aachen and Ryan's Son had two four-fault rounds, and both were as good as named for the squad when asked to rest their horses until the final Olympic trial in Cardiff, where they were so dominant that team manager Ronnie Massarella announced that they were "definitely in. "

But fate intervened. It was decided that all the possible Montreal-bound horses should compete over an Olympic size course at Hickstead. Moxy, consistent as ever, came through the test with flying colours but Ryan's Son resolutely refused to jump the double before the water, and nothing John tried could persuade him over it. So Ryan's Son stayed at home, and quickly resumed a victorious path that went on for years, while the gallant Moxy had everything drained out of him in the quagmire that was the Bromont show jumping arena.

Thunder and lightning and non-stop torrential rain made the huge course almost unjumpable, except for Alwin Schockemöhle's Warwick Rex: they jumped clear twice but no one else could manage that even once, and in the end three jumped off for the silver and bronze. Moxy, brave as ever, was among them, but now even he had had enough, and tired to finish fourth.

He was never as good again, while Ryan's Son was at the top for most of the next decade.

STROLLER

To have witnessed Stroller show jumping is akin to having watched Arkle in steeplechasing; both transcended from sports news to front pages; Stroller was an English icon and Arkle an Irish one but both went much further than their national boundaries.

Stroller was a pony. As such, he was a star pony jumper. But even though JA ponies, the highest grade, are champions at that level, it was virtually unheard of for a pony to progress to horse classes. For one thing, the distances between fences would be gauged for a horse's length of stride, not a pony's; and for another even a JA pony could not be expected to jump the full-size horse courses, at least not at the top level and especially not at Olympic level.

So Stroller, like Arkle, was a freak. Good looking with a white star, and so athletic he looked the model of miniature thoroughbred, he came from Ireland along with a number of others to Sussex dealer Tommy Grantham. He was by a thoroughbred, possibly Little Heaven, the sire of one of Ireland's smallest top show jumpers, Dundrum, and was out of a Connemara pony mare. He was sold to a local butcher for his daughter to show jump and from there to the Coakes family in Hampshire, where two brothers, John and Douglas, were already members of the British junior show-jumping team. Douglas was part of the British gold-medal winning team of the 1960 Junior European Championships in Venice. Little could the brothers have guessed then that their little sister Marion would eclipse them and take global show jumping by storm.

Marion was 13 years old and Stroller was 8. By the time she was 16 and due to come out of juniors, the normal route would have been to sell Stroller to another up-and-coming junior and move on to horses herself. Among their junior successes together had been a junior European team gold in Berlin in 1962, and team silver in Budapest in 1964. (In the intervening year Marion won another junior European team gold in Rotterdam on a pony called Spring Shandy.)

Ann Moore, three years Marion's junior and who was also to win an Olympic silver medal in Munich just four years after Marion and Stroller in Mexico, actually tried Stroller – but Marion was adamant that she wanted to register him for horse classes, and persuaded her father to do just that.

The relatively new Hickstead was not far from where the Coakes family farmed in Hampshire and the All-England Jumping course became a regular stamping ground. Stroller was 'leading horse' there for five consecutive years, 1965 to 1970, but more than that, he became a Hickstead Derby specialist; he finished second at his first attempt in 1964 to the great Seamus Hayes and Goodbye.

Three years later Stroller was the Derby victor: he was the only one out of forty-four starters to achieve a clear round, keeping his feet in a stumble and slide down the big bank. He was also second in 1968, and third in 1970.

When she was 18 in 1965, Marion rode Stroller to triumph in the ladies' World Championship at Hickstead, beating strong opposition over three days. That year, Marion and Stroller captured the Queen Elizabeth Cup at the Royal International, and they won it again six years later.

In only his second season as a senior show jumper, Stroller helped Britain to win three Nations Cups, and the President's Cup, the World Championships for teams.

Incredibly, Stroller also included Puissance in his repertoire. His last appearance in one was at the Antwerp show in 1967. He cleared the wall at 6ft 8in, and only put a brick out at 6ft 10in, to win jointly with Alwin Schockemöhle on Athlet, a great Puissance specialist.

And so, in spite of his small size, Stroller had a big record and was selected for the 1968 Mexico Olympics. It turned into a story of glory and disaster. A number of the foreign horses were affected by the high altitude, but added to that poor Stroller suffered from a broken and decayed tooth, which caused him a horrific toothache that will be understood by any human who has gone through it.

Nevertheless, Stroller jumped like only he could, and went clear over the huge course in the first round of the individual contest. There were no clears in the massive second round, and Stroller collected eight faults. Only one combination did better than that; America's Bill Steinkraus and Snowbound knocked one fence for four faults, and with it took the gold medal. Stroller and Marion were the next closest, so took silver.

But the team event turned into disaster for him and what happened was worse than seeing Arkle limping in, beaten in his last race because of a broken pedal bone. Stroller was in pain with the tooth abscess. For the sake of Britain they jumped in the team event. Stroller had the one and only stop in his life, refusing the first of the two parallels. But worse than that, when he re-attempted it he refused again and fell into it. Little Stroller in a tangle of poles on the ground. They were out of the time allowed and eliminated.

Later that year, Marion Coakes was named Sportswoman of the Year.

Perhaps the most remarkable thing of all, and testament to Stroller's incredible guts and inimitable personality, is that his career continued on as if that Mexican debacle had never happened. It is hard to believe, but in 1970, at 20 years old, he won the mighty Hamburg Derby with the only clear round; it was just the fiftieth clear in the event's history, and the first by a woman. Stroller was also second in the Hickstead Derby, and was Leading Show Jumper of the Year at the Horse of the Year Show that autumn.

Even then his career was not quite over. In 1971, Stroller and Marion won Hickstead's British Championship, eleven years after he appeared at the first Hickstead show (with his previous owner). Altogether, Stroller won sixty-one international competitions.

In 1969 Marion married David Mould, jockey to National Hunt trainer Peter Cazelet at Fairlawne, Kent, from where he rode many winners for the Queen Mother.

In the early 1970s Stroller retired to the farm in Hampshire where he lived for fifteen years until he died of a heart attack at the venerable age of 36.

5

PRINCIPAL SHOWS

HORSE OF THE YEAR SHOW

The accolade 'Horse of the Year' is the aim of equestrian riders throughout Britain, and the pinnacle for the winners of any given category. It covers not only all levels of senior and junior show jumping, but also show classes for horses and ponies.

The brainchild of Captain Tony Collings, who felt there should be a climax to each season to produce a champion of champions show, it was taken up by Colonel Sir Michael Ansell and Colonel V.D.S. Williams (father of commentator Dorian Williams). As it would be held in the autumn it would need to be indoors and so Colonels Ansell and Williams visited the indoor 'Le Jumping' show in Paris. Never before had they seen audience participation and reaction like it.

They negotiated the Harringay greyhound track as a venue; the BSJA organised the show-jumping side and Tony Collings ran the show classes. The concept worked, with both jumpers and show horses qualifying for HOYS (as the Horse of the Year Show became known) at various shows throughout the country during the year.

Its first show, in 1949, attracted 400 entries, and a horse or pony of the year for each section was crowned in front of an enthusiastic crowd. Ten years later it moved to Wembley Arena where it remained for four decades until, in 2002, it moved to central England, to the NEC Arena, Birmingham, set in 50 acres. The move away from London may have been a risk, but the gamble paid off, and today there are likely to be more than 1,500 competitors and some 65,000 spectators. Its culmination is a final evening gala performance which traditionally ends with a cavalcade and a rendering of the Ode to the Horse (written for the show in 1964 by Devon poet Ronald Duncan at the request of Colonel Ansell).

THE ROYAL INTERNATIONAL HORSE SHOW

Like the Horse of the Year Show, the Royal International is also a mix of show jumping and showing classes; it is the flagship of the British Horse Society. This is the show that was staged originally in Olympia in 1907 by the BHS forerunner, the Institute of the Horse and Pony Club, which makes it the oldest horse show in Great Britain. The First World War saw its discontinuance until 1933, when the 10th Duke of Beaufort revived it. (He was also to offer his estate, Badminton, for three-day-eventing after watching the event at the 1948 Olympic Games in London, at which two British riders finished an unimpressive seventeenth and twenty-seventh of forty-five, and the third rider was among twelve who did not finish.)

The Royal International Horse Show has had a few homes since Olympia; it was staged at Wembley and White City in London, and at

DID YOU KNOW?

The RDS Arena in Ballsbridge, Dublin, is not exclusively used by the annual horse show. In 1983, the Ireland tennis team played in the World Group of the Davis Cup for the only time. The match against a United States team including John McEnroe was played in the RDS rather than the usual venue, Fitzwilliam, to accommodate crowds of 6,000 each day. It is also home to Leinster Rugby and venue for rock concerts.

Anxious lest the Customs officials should confiscate her newly won trophies on a trip to Geneva in 1949, Pat Smythe debated whether to declare them or try to conceal them: a mounted clock with silver horseshoes on the hands, a silver compact, and a light tin cup on a heavy marble base. Honesty won, and the Customs officer waved her through with a kind comment. It was her 21st birthday.

the NEC Centre in Birmingham, but since 1992 the All-England Jumping Course at Hickstead, Sussex, has been home to the six-day show.

The jumping includes the UK's only Nations Cup, a qualifier for the World Championships in which the final four riders all ride each other's horses.

The Queen Elizabeth II Cup remains one of the most coveted titles on the national show-jumping circuit, in spite of its demotion to national from international class, and the Sunday finale is the King George V Gold Cup, one of the oldest and most prestigious titles in the show jumping world, and since 2008 open to women as well as men.

The show also stages many national show-jumping classes, as well as carriage driving, scurry driving, side-saddle classes and many showing classes, including those for the Supreme Horse and Supreme Pony Championships.

THE RDS DUBLIN HORSE SHOW

Dublin, as we have already seen, was the birthplace of show jumping, and it follows that it is the oldest show in Great Britain or Ireland staging the sport. Today, its permanent 44-acre site in Ballsbridge is always abuzz with colour, atmosphere and majestic horses and ponies both showing and jumping during the Wednesday to Sunday of its show early every August.

In addition to the main arena, there are two show rings, 1 and 2, which lie between the Anglesea stand and the main permanent buildings and the stabling area and clock tower which acts as an unofficial meeting point for visitors. The buildings house a huge array of trade stands.

The showing classes for horses and ponies take place in these rings and draw their own aficionados to spectate. The champions from the various classes are decided in the main arena, and then take part in the Champions of the Show parade which is a magnificent spectacle currently in the early afternoon of Sunday, the last day of the show.

For the show jumpers, Simmonscourt lies across the Simmonscourt Road from the main arena and plays host to many of the supporting or qualifying show-jumping classes during the week, along with several aisles of trade stands; the Pavilion itself is also used for trade exhibitions during the year.

Dublin Horse Show first held a Grand Prix in 1934 for the Irish trophy and was won by Commandant J.D. (Jed) O'Dwyer of the Army Equitation School. The first timed jumping competition was held in 1938, and in 1951 an electric clock was installed, since when a time factor has entered most competitions. There was no Nations Cup held in 1952 due to the Olympic Games.

In 1976, after fifty years of international competition, the two grass banks in the Arena were removed so the arena could be used for other events. The continental band at the western end of the main arena was added later.

Shows have been held annually except from 1914 to 1919 due to the First World War and from 1940 to 1946 due to the Second World War.

In 2003 the Nations Cup Competition for the Aga Khan Trophy became part of the Samsung Super League under the auspices of the Fédération Equestre Internationale (the FEI). In 2013 the Nations Cup Competition for the Aga Khan Trophy became part of the Furusiyya FEI Nations Cup Series.

With the world's top jumpers taking part, prize money among the most generous anywhere, and an atmosphere and social milieu beyond any, the RDS remains at the top of the tree for competitors and spectators alike.

THE OLYMPICS

'Prize jumping' for high jump and long jump became an equestrian discipline at the 1900 Olympic Games in Paris, the second games of the modern Olympiad and the first in which women were allowed to compete. Twenty-four riders from Belgium, France, Italy and the USA took part. It was not until the 1912 Stockholm Olympics that a Nations Cup style show-jumping event was staged. Great Britain first took part in 1924, in Paris, and finished seventh of eight teams. They first won a medal, Bronze, at the 1948 Games in London behind Mexico and Spain, with Harry Llewellyn on Foxhunter, Henry Nicoll on Kilgeddin and Arthur Carr on Monty. No less than eleven of the fourteen teams were eliminated, including Ireland.

Great Britain built on its third place four years later by winning the Gold Medal with Foxhunter, Wilf White on Nizefela and Duggie Stewart on Aherlow. Four years later it was Bronze again for GB, with Nizefela, Pat Smythe on Flanagan and Peter Robeson on Scorchin. Ireland figured for the first time, finishing seventh of twenty teams.

So to those London Olympic Games in 2012. If there was ever the belief that a home side has an advantage, through sheer national support, it was proved now for all the equestrian disciplines, but especially for the show-jumping team.

When I was young, Britain was not just a poor relation at dressage, it was more like a foreign language with no interest to learn it. It was for sissies; being good at crossing a challenging landscape behind a pack of flying hounds was far more the thing. That began to change with the

HORSE HUMOUR

Q) What animal has more hands than feet?
A) Why, a horse, of course!

necessity to perform a reasonable dressage test in three-day eventing – but if anyone had predicted that within a few decades Britain would hold a gold medal in Olympic dressage, they would have been laughed out of court.

However, in London 2012, Britain did just that, through the extraordinary talent of Charlotte Dujardin, her long-time trainer and for many years Britain's only top-flight dressage exponent Carl Hester, and an incredible horse, Valegro. And, what's more, Britain had three riders in the top five, including the bronze. These three, Charlotte, Carl, and Laura Bechtolsheimer also won the team gold for Great Britain.

The British three-day event team had a much better track record; they had won gold in Stockholm 1956, Mexico 1968 and Munich 1972, and had collected many silver and bronze medals in the interim. Individual medals had been won down through the years, including gold in Munich (Richard Meade) and Athens (Leslie Law, 2004), so they could reasonably be expected to do well in London. The team of Nicola Wilson, Mary King, Zara Phillips, Kristina Cook and William Fox-Pitt took silver.

But the only previous time the British show-jumping squad had won gold had been sixty years before, in Helsinki 1952; the team also won bronze in London 1948, Stockholm 1956, and silver in Los Angeles 1984. David Broome was the first Briton to win an individual medal for Great Britain in show jumping, a bronze in Rome 1960, followed by another bronze in Mexico in 1968 when Marion Mould won silver with Stroller. In between, in Tokyo 1964, Peter Robeson had won bronze, and then the silver medal won by Ann Moore in Munich 1972 was the last show-jumping medal of any hue won by Britain until forty years later, in London 2012, in a thrilling finish that went down to the last British rider in a two-team jump-off.

DID YOU KNOW?

David Broome remains the only British rider to have won the World Championship. He achieved it in La Baule in 1970 on Beethoven, a brilliant but temperamental horse. Beethoven was owned and originally ridden by Douglas Bunn; he was second in the 1965 King George V Gold Cup, but was sometimes eliminated in lesser competitions for three refusals. Bunn offered the ride to Broome, and even five years later it was a big gamble to take him in the World Championships. Bunn was *chef d'équipe* of the British team as well as Beethoven's owner, and he took the gamble.

David Broome, a first-rate, lifelong ambassador for the sport and, in 2013 president of the British Showjumping Association, had hoped to ride the ultra-reliable Mister Softee. The combination had twice previously won the European Championships, in 1967 and 1969, and had taken a bronze medal in the 1968 Mexico Olympics, but by the time of the 1970 World Championships Mister Softee was 18 and considered in some quarters to be too old. That left David with the choice of Beethoven, who might refuse but had the ability to win, or Top of the Morning, who was consistent but unlikely to be good enough to win.

In the event, Beethoven was on his best behaviour – even for the other three riders in the final, when, under the unique World Championship formula, all four riders rode their own and their rivals' horses.

When it was German rider Alwin Schockemöhle's turn to ride Beethoven, he was half a stride wrong approaching the third element of the treble, and could easily have jacked it in, but instead sailed through.

Bunn, watching with Broome, said, 'The rotten old devil, fancy him doing that!'

The liver chestnut Irish-bred Beethoven was by a thoroughbred, Roi d'Egypte out of an Irish draught mare called Fanny; he was bought as an unbroken 3-year-old in 1961 by Jack Bamber, a Northern Ireland dealer.

The first two main rounds of the competition had come before that. Peter Charles' horse, Vindicat, was not considered as good as his three teammates, and he then fluffed his lines by being too strung up and excited by the audience and the occasion, knocking up the discard score.

After this first round 'new boys' Saudi Arabia held the lead, with England lying second and Holland close behind.

Next day, for round two, Nick Skelton on Big Star had a clear round and Ben Maher had four faults with Triple X, which put the team ahead of Saudi Arabia. Scott Brash then went clear on Hello Sanctos, and finally Peter Charles' Vindicat had one fence down for four faults, plus a time penalty. This meant the possible winners now were Holland. All that their last rider, Gerco Schroder, had to do was jump clear and the gold medal was theirs. But his horse (called London!) incurred four faults, forcing a jump-off between the two nations to decide the gold medal.

Now came the real nail-biting stuff. Nick Skelton on Big Star and Ben Maher on Triple X both went clear for Britain. But so did the first Dutch rider. Their second, however, knocked two fences for eight faults. Both Scott Brash and the next Dutch rider had just one fence down, for four faults. If – if – Peter Charles and his horse Vindicat could go clear, Britain would win. In they came to the stunning Greenwich, London Arena. They were in no hurry. A steady clear was their aim. They achieved it – and the Olympic Gold medal for show jumping went to Great Britain for the first time in six decades.

6

SHOW JUMPING IN LITERATURE

MASTER OF ONE

An autobiography by Dorian Williams (J.M. Dent & Sons, 1978), this is one of my favourite books, beautifully written and illustrating Dorian Williams' life as a true all-round gentleman, and also one with considerable humour. It details not only his panache as a show-jumping commentator, but also his passion for hunting (he was Master of the Whaddon Chase) and his love of Shakespeare which led to him founding the outdoor theatre at Pendley, Hertfordshire. He also wrote *Pendley and a Pack of Hounds* describing these latter two life involvements. His small book *Lost*, about his missing terrier, is told with pathos and emotion. He also wrote a number of children's pony stories as well as several show-jumping books. Dorian, a former prep school headmaster and an old Harrovian, always had time for a person, even if there was someone 'more important' nearby.

It is largely thanks to him that show jumping became a mainstream TV sport in the 1970s, and up until his final broadcast at the Olympia Horse Show in 1985 he was 'the voice of show jumping'.

He was chairman of the British Horse Society, and instrumental in setting up the National Equestrian Centre (NEC) at Stoneleigh Abbey in Warwickshire. In 2005, he was one of the inaugural laureates appointed to the British Horse Society Equestrian Hall of Fame.

RIDERS

By Jilly Cooper, this is a rollicking, frolicking, all the racey storytelling one has come to expect from Jilly – and her list of acknowledgements reads like a veritable who's who of show jumping. This was the first of her 'Rutshire Chronicles', and those that followed were roughly more of the same, covering different equine themes.

SHOW JUMPING SECRET

I loved all the Pullein-Thompson books, and have chosen this one, by Josephine, published by Armada in 1969, for its show jumping title. They were written by three sisters, Josephine and twins Christine and Diana. Reading them today they sound so outdated yet remain utterly charming – and, of course, they were good stories, and that stands the test of time. Josephine Pullein-Thompson died in 2014.

SHOW JUMPING, RECORDS, FACTS AND CHAMPIONS

A treasure trove of facts, figures and anecdotes, Judith Draper's book (published by Guinness Books in 1987) is largely superseded today by access to the internet, yet it is a pleasure to hold such a volume in one's hands and dip into it. Judith was an accomplished and meticulous equestrian journalist and a reliable source for any researcher, pleasure reader or argument solver.

Judith also wrote *The Stars of Show Jumping* (Stanley Paul, 1990), which gives portraits of twenty-five of the world's top show-jumping riders of the day. This includes the Whitaker brothers, John and Michael; Smith father and sons, Harvey, and Robert and Steven; and siblings David Broome and Liz Edgar, among others for the UK; Eddie Macken for Ireland, and also stars from abroad such as Brazilian Nelson Pessoa; Franke Sloothaak from Holland; and Austrian Thomas Fruhmann, as well as a chapter devoted to 'The Americans'.

THE EDGARS FOREVER

By Ann Martin and published by Pelham Books in 1984, this is an entertaining read as well as being informative about show jumping in general and the Edgar stable in particular, with behind-the-scenes glimpses of the sport. It includes some hard-hitting views on some of the rules and regulations, as well as many amusing anecdotes about Ted and Liz (*née* Broome) Edgar, their principle rider at the time Nick Skelton, their up-and-coming newly-senior rider Lesley McNaught, and their own young protégée Marie Edgar.

There was the time Ted was kicked and dislocated his elbow as he was about to head off for Hickstead. He stopped in London en route to have it put back in but the swelling was so great he couldn't get his shirt on. Douglas Bunn, Master of Hickstead, offered him a crate of champagne if he could complete the Hickstead Derby. Riding one-handed, with his other arm in a sling, Ted Edgar did just that, an amazing feat.

Ann Martin's chapter on Nick Skelton begins, '"If," Liz is wont to say, "Ted could order a son, it would be Nick".' After Nick first came over with his pony for sorting out (when his ambition was still to be a jockey), it was Liz Edgar who helped him. That evening Ted asked her what the pony was like. Ann Martin wrote, 'Liz, who has the same flair for detecting embryo talent that Ted demonstrates in his purchases of novice horses (like a ferret in search of a rabbit), replied, "The pony was useless, but I think the kid is brilliant. He reminded me of my brother in the old days. There was something I had to like, he had so much natural ability."'

The partnership lasted many years but was not without its low points and in 1985 he went out on is own.

Lesley McNaught was an outstanding Junior and then Young Rider who also received great help from the Edgars. Ann Martin wrote that in March 1983, Lesley said, 'I have learnt so much from Ted and Liz, but one point that stands out is Ted's advice on shows: "Do your own thing and don't listen to collecting ring prattle".'

Liz was very good at teaching on the ground, and Ted was likely to get on a horse to demonstrate a point.

This book is an excellent and interesting read, and can be dipped in and out of.

HARVEY SMITH

Harvey Smith has a number of show jumping books to his name, sometimes with an acknowledged co-author. These are the best-known ones:

Harvey Smith on Show Jumping, Harvey Smith and Victor Green (Pelham Books, 1984)
Harvey (White Lion Publishers, 1977)
Harvesting Success (Pelham Books, 1968)
Bedside Jumping (Collins, 1985)
V is for Victory (William Kimber & Co. Ltd, 1972)

GENEVIEVE MURPHY

Genevieve Murphy is a long-established national equestrian correspondent, and she has co-written a number of books with high-profile riders, and under her own name alone she has *The Facts About Show Jumping* (Fact Books, Andre Deutsch, 1979), featuring Eddie Macken and his horses.

JUMPING THE ODDS: MEMOIRS OF A RASTAFARIAN SHOWJUMPER

This autobiography of Oliver Skeete, published in 1996, describes how he progressed from a wild life of partying and petty crime in the backstreets of London to being Britain's first black show jumper, even though he did not begin to ride until he was 35 years old.

KING OF DIAMONDS: AN IRISH SHOW JUMPING DYNASTY

Nicholas O'Hare, from County Meath, is a prolific author of books about the Irish sport horse, including two of Ireland's top show jumping sires, King of Diamonds (Nicholas O'Hare, 2001) and Clover Hill (*Clover Hill: His Life and Legacy*, Nicholas O'Hare, 2008.) Two very different horses but with one influence: for the good of the breed that produces top Irish show jumpers and both have founded long lines of successful progeny. King of Diamonds goes down as a foundation sire of the Irish Sport Horse. Clover Hill was half thoroughbred but he made his stamp on Irish breeding and his blood runs in many great show jumpers.

SHOW-JUMPING GUIDES

Show Jumping by Jane Wallace (Threshold Picture Guide, Kenilworth Press) 2006 and *Solving Show-Jumping Problems*, same author and publisher 1998, are short (twenty-four pages) easy to follow illustrated guides for would-be show jumpers and as such they are invaluable.

QUOTES AND SAYINGS

'The air of heaven is that which blows through a horse's ears.' – Arabic proverb

'Show me your horse and I will show you what you are.' – British saying

'No one can teach riding so well as a horse.' – C.S. Lewis

'A canter is the cure for all evils.' – Benjamin Disraeli

'Dear to me is my bonny white steed; Oft has he helped me at pinch of need.' – Sir Walter Scott

'There is no secret so close as that between a rider and his horse.' – R.S. Surtees

'A good horse should be seldom spurred.' – Thomas Fuller

'Hast thou given the horse strength? Has thou clothed his neck with thunder?' – Job 39:19

'O, for a horse with wings!' – Shakespeare

'Horses and poets should be fed, not overfed.' – Charles IX

'His mane is like a river flowing, And his eyes like embers glowing in the darkness of night, And his pace swift as light.' – Bryan Waller Procter

'I will not change my horses with any that treads but on four pasterns. / When I bestride him, I soar, I am a hawk. / He trots the air. / The earth sings when he touches it.' – Shakespeare

'The horse, the horse! / The symbol of surging potency and power of movement, of action, in man.' – D.H. Lawrence

'I heard a neigh, oh, such a brisk and melodious neigh it was. My very heart leaped with the sound.' – Nathaniel Hawthorne

'For want of a nail the shoe is lost, for want of a shoe the horse is lost, for want of a horse the rider is lost.' – George Herbert

'Take the life of cities! Here's the life for me. 'Twere a thousand pities not to gallop free.' – Anonymous

'Now a polo pony [show jumper] is like a poet. If he is born with a love for the game, he can be made.' – Rudyard Kipling

'God forbid that I should go to any heaven in which there are no horses.' – Robert Brontine Cunninghame-Graham

'To many, the words love, hope, and dreams are synonymous with horses.' – Oliver Wendell Holmes

'It is not best to swap horses while crossing the river.' – Abraham Lincoln (1864)

'The best horse doesn't always win the race.' – Irish proverb

'Horse sense is the thing a horse has which keeps it from betting on people.' – W.C. Fields

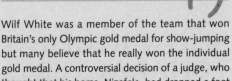

DID YOU KNOW?

Wilf White was a member of the team that won Britain's only Olympic gold medal for show-jumping but many believe that he really won the individual gold medal. A controversial decision of a judge, who thought that his horse, Nizefela, had dropped a foot in the water, left White officially with four faults in fifth place.

Sir Harry Llewellyn, who was also on the victorious team, was always convinced that Nizefela cleared the water. 'It was not considered "British" to complain and so no objection was lodged,' Llewellyn wrote in his autobiography. 'I think to this day that Wilf White is the unluckiest man I have ever known not to have won an individual gold medal.'

'If wishes were horses, beggars might ride.' – John Ray

'The sturdy steed now goes to grass and they hang up his saddle.' – Francis Beaumont

'Spur not an unbroken horse; put not your plowshare too deep into new ground.' – Sir Walter Scott

'Spare the lash, my boy, and hold the reins more firmly!' – Ovid

'Ride not a free horse to death.' – Miguel Cervantes

7

SHOW-JUMPING CHARACTERS

SHOW-JUMPING CORRESPONDENT

Alan Smith was show-jumping correspondent to the *Daily Telegraph* for forty-eight years, from 1960 until 2008. He also covered skiing for the paper each winter for thirty-four years.

As a lifelong horse-racing enthusiast, it was in that field that he began reporting with the *Sheffield Telegraph* in 1958, covering the northern meetings, along with the one-eyed Ken Ellis. But Fleet Street beckoned, even though it was reporting on show hunters that he started with the *Daily Telegraph*. At the time, Peter Scott was Hotspur (the racing tipster) and John Lawrence (later Lord Oaksey) had just joined.

The first show Alan Smith covered was the annual Finmere Charity Show, Oxfordshire, held in aid of Stoke Mandeville Hospital, renowned for treating spinal injuries (this was prior to the Injured Jockeys Fund). In 1961 Alan Smith covered the Junior European Show Jumping Championships at the year-old Hickstead. The following year Alan asked his sports editor, Kingsley Wright, if he should cover them for 1962.

'Did you do so last year?'

'Yes.'

'Then we must cover them again.'

They were to be held that year in Berlin, and so began a career that took Alan literally round the world. He could often take his wife, Maddy, and sometimes their three children, too. He has reported on, and got to know, the greats of the sport, as well as having seen huge changes.

In 1965, octogenarian Arnie Lunn retired from skiing-reporting for the *Daily Telegraph* and Alan, an occasional skier, stepped in; at this time, show jumping was still a summer-only sport. On his first winter assignment, Alan found himself staying in the hotel in St Moritz, which was at the top of the bob run, where all the bobbers were staying. He covered every Winter Olympics for thirty years and the summer ones for forty-eight years, i.e. twelve separate show-jumping Olympics.

HORSE HUMOUR

Horse sales terminology:

BOLD: runaway.
GOOD MOVER: runaway.
ATHLETIC: runaway.
NEEDS INTERMEDIATE RIDER: runaway.

'I've led a charmed life, you couldn't invent a better job,' he says. And for good measure, in retirement, he is a part-owner in a few successful racehorses.

Here, he retells just some of his memorable show-jumping stories:

Ann Moore

Ann Moore found she had officials to beat as well as her rivals in 1973, when she and her silver Olympic medallist Psalm travelled to Vienna to defend their Women's European Championship.

Ann and Caroline Bradley, with True Lass, arrived in the Austrian capital after a long road journey, and, discovering that there was to be no warm-up competition for the championship, decided to go in the opening, non-championship event. But none of the German or Belgium riders had entered, so the judges, under the chairmanship of Belgian José Hoffman, decided no one should be allowed to do so, under penalty of being disqualified from the championships if they did.

The two British women were walking the course when a British official discovered what the jury had decided, warned them, and they withdrew. Hoffman had seen them on the course but said afterwards he did not think it his duty to tell them of the threat of disqualification. 'They should know the rules,' he said – even though the rule had just been made up – 'if they had started, we would have disqualified them.'

Whilst there may have been some people happy to see the riders excluded, thankfully this did not come to pass. Ann retained her title, with Caroline coming in second.

Tina Cassan

Tina Cassan also found herself battling officialdom in the 1992 final of the World Cup in Del Mar, California, when, as she cantered Genesis round before the start of the opening speed leg, she noticed the clock had already started and had clocked up twenty seconds. The starting line was so wide that she had inadvertently crossed it. The vastly more experienced Ludger Beerbaum had done the same, but for him this was only noticed when he finished in an absurdly long time. The eagle-eyed Tina stopped and pointed to the clock, but was told to go on anyway, and when she refused she was told she had been eliminated and should leave the ring. The crowd, realising she had been ill-treated, loudly booed the judges and urged her to stay in the ring; she did, and after a fifteen-minute stand-off was told she could start again, though with no guarantee her round would count. But afterwards the jury of appeal decided 'in the best overall interest of the sport' that her round should count and Beerbaum's time should be amended.

Merely-A-Monarch

Few horses have proved more versatile than Anneli Drummond-Hay's Merely-A-Monarch. After she won the first running of the Burghley three-day event in 1961, and Badminton the following spring, Anneli's thoughts turned to the 1964 Tokyo Olympic Games. But there was a snag: women at that time, 1962, were not allowed to compete in the Olympic three-day event, and so she turned her attention to show jumping, with immediate success. Within weeks the pair was not only show jumping at the highest level, but they also won the Imperial Cup at the Royal International Horse Show. A year later the combination finished third to Pat Smythe in the European Championships.

Ironically, in 1964, when the rule was changed and women were allowed in to the Olympic three-day event, Merely-A-Monarch fell ill, and he was not able to compete in the show jumping. In fact, it was 1967 before he came back to form, winning the Geneva Grand Prix. The great National Hunt trainer Fulke Walwyn reckoned he could have won the Grand National at Aintree.

Anneli Drummond-Hay, who began her career as an eventer, also won the 1969 Hickstead Derby with her ex-hunt horse Xanthos.

Another show-jumping veteran, course-designer and five-times national champion Alan Oliver, also retired after more than sixty years in the sport.

DID YOU KNOW?

Two stalwart ambassadors of show jumping retired within weeks of each other in 2000. British show-jumping team's *chef d'équipe* Ronnie Massarella retired after the Rome Nations Cup final in October. The Italian-born Yorkshireman became a permanent *chef d'équipe* in 1970 and had presided over eight Olympic teams.

The winner of the 2014 Hickstead Derby had only one eye. Karen Swann's bay gelding Adventure De Kannan, ridden by Ireland's Trevor Breen, held off the previous year's champion, British rider Phillip Miller on the grey stallion Caritiar Z, by two hundredths of a second in a jump-off after both horses collected four faults in the first round. Adventure de Kannan had an eye removed during surgery in 2013 following a five-year-long eye condition.

Althea Roger Smith

Althea Roger Smith, a leading show jumper who went on to marry champion National Hunt jockey then trainer Josh Gifford, would be reading books in a caravan while the rest were boozing. 'She was such a favourite of our three children, especially our daughter Charlotte; there was a show in Wiltshire and Caroline had a dozen horses but when she saw Charlotte she hopped off to chat.'

Ronnie Massarella

Ronnie Massarella was British team manager for twenty years, but more than that, he was also a friend to all those involved in the sport. In December 2000 the show-jumping world honoured him at Olympia with awards in recognition of his service. He did sterling work for the British team, always, it seemed, with a smile – and he never asked for expenses. In addition, he thought nothing of paying for wining and dining those around him. There was the occasion of his eightieth birthday when he took a number of people out to dinner in Aachen. Some of the women, expecting to be 'a deux' with him, were spread among the rest of guests.

While he was at the helm of the British team, Britain won the Aga Khan Cup four times during the 1980s. Since then the magnificent gold trophy has taken pride of place at the British Showjumping Association's headquarters in Stoneleigh, Warwickshire.

When Britain won the competition on another three consecutive occasions in the 1990s, Massarella expected to keep the trophy. However, it had to be returned to Ireland when a team horse was drug tested positively.

This was an incident I recorded in *Drugs and Horses* (Compass Equestrian, 2000):

> Nowadays manufacturers are fastidious not only with their ingredients but also with the cleanliness of their machinery and the environment in which the fodder is produced. It is also labelled as being free from prohibited substances. The odd case can 'slip through the net' as happened with Great Britain's triumphant Nations Cup team when winning the prestigious Aga Khan Trophy at the Royal Dublin Show in the early 1990s. The team had won it the previous two years and so time-honoured team manager Ronnie Massarella could reasonably expect to take the trophy back to England permanently after the team's outright hat-trick. But David Broome, OBE, one of the sport's all-time greats as both rider and ambassador, and with Olympic, World and European medals to his name, suffered the ignominy and embarrassment of his horse, Lannegan, being positively dope tested.
>
> A minute trace of a banned substance, isoxoprene, a drug which helps thin the blood (bringing relief in cases of navicular) was detected in a supply of electrolytes. 'The result was like a bolt out of the blue,' says David. 'Any injections our horses have are given through our vet, and Lannegan never had navicular.'
>
> As luck would have it, David still had the electrolytes container and it was sent away for examination. It turned out that a shovel used for the electrolytes had previously been used for handling isoxoprene. The amount found in the drug test was one/four-hundreds of a single dose. But it was a positive test. The horse was disqualified. And England lost not only that year's Aga Khan Nations Cup but also the right to hold the trophy permanently.
>
> The only good thing about the case was that, when it realised what had happened, the drugs company concerned 'put its hands

up', paid all the expenses concerned with the case including the fine, and even paid the team the prize money it would have won. 'They were so honest about it that I won't even name them,' says David now, 'but it had been an exceptionally good competition. After the first horse had been in the second round we were 20 faults adrift, yet we drew level and forced a jump-off, which we then won. Coming from so far behind, it was the most wonderful cup to win,' he recalls as if it was yesterday.

Ronnie Massarella's grandfather, Giovanni, started life in Italy as a farm labourer, but he moved to the north of England to try and improve himself; one of the ventures he embarked on was selling ice cream from the back of the cart (another was performing on a home-made barrel organ).

At the height of success in the 1950s, Massarellas was producing 5,000 gallons of ice cream a day, becoming one of the biggest ice cream manufacturers in Europe. The company was sold to J Lyons in the 1950s, but in 1963 Giovanni's grandson, Ronnie, bought back part of the retailing business, which would become one of the country's leading ice cream retailers, including in due course Mister Softee (as in the great showjumper ridden by David Broome). In 2014, at the age of 91, Ronnie Massarella and his company celebrated 150 years of the company from his home and headquarters, Thurcroft Hall, near Sheffield; only his wife, Edna Elizabeth was missing, having died in 2012 at the age of 86.

8

MAJOR TROPHIES

THE KING GEORGE V GOLD CUP AND THE QUEEN ELIZABETH II CUP

The King George V Gold Cup is almost as old as show jumping itself, dating from Olympia in 1911, when it was won by Dimitri d'Exe from Russia riding Picollo. It was the top men's individual competition in England, and from the start it had an international flavour.

The Queen Elizabeth II Cup for lady riders began in 1949 (as the Princess Elizabeth Cup) at White City as part of the Royal International Horse Show. It was won by the great Irish rider and instructor Iris Kellet on her super horse Rusty for a prize of £30. Both trophies were highly sought after and were their respective gender pinnacles. But in 2008 sex equality reared its head. The Queen's Cup was downgraded from international to national and opened up to men as well as women. In the same stroke, women became eligible to contest the King George V Gold Cup.

Prize money for the Queen's Cup was always less than for the King George; such is life. In recent times it was £6,000 for the ladies, while the men's equivalent was two and a half times as much at £15,000.

Show jumping is an equal sport between the sexes; there is no differentiation in ability. In horse racing, which also has the horse as 50 per cent of the whole component, female professional riders (few as they are) receive the same money as their male counterparts, and quite rightly so.

In show jumping, both the King George and the Queen Elizabeth cups are run at the Royal International Horse Show, Hickstead in July. In 2008, in the first running under its new, either-sex guise, the 'ladies'' cup was won by Ireland's Shane Breen. The King George had to wait until 2014 for a lady rider to win, when Beezie Madden took the coveted trophy home to America.

The winners of both cups over the years read like a who's who of show jumping. After the Russian winner in 1911, the King George V Gold Cup went to Belgium and three times to France before Geoffrey

Brooke won it for Britain in 1921 (there was no contest from 1915 to 1919 because of First World War). The trophy went to America in 1926. Jack Talbot-Ponsonby won it for Britain in 1930, '32 and '33, and then it was Ireland's turn in 1934 and '35 with John Lewis and Jed O'Dwyer. There was no contest between 1940 and 1946 because of the Second World War, and soon after that Colonel Sir Harry Llewellyn and his mighty Foxhunter came into their own, winning the coveted trophy in 1948, '50 and '53.

The first of David Broome's record-breaking six wins came in 1960 with Sunsalve, followed in 1966 with Mister Softee. It was his turn again in 1972 with Sportsman, and 1977 with Philco. His winner in the 1980s was Mr Ross (1981) and incredibly, a decade later he won the great prize for a sixth time, in 1991, with Lannegan.

The news in 2008 that the Queen Elizabeth Cup was to be downgraded to a national class and opened up to both sexes was greeted with dismay by traditionalists. Five-times winner Liz Edgar (wife of Ted Edgar and sister of David Broome) confessed she was appalled by the decision.

She told *Horse and Hound*, 'It is the best cup in England to win for the lady riders, something really special. If they couldn't continue to run it as it was at Hickstead, they should have put it into another competition.'

But she added that the competition had always been let down by the poor prize money on offer in comparison to the men's equivalent class, the King George V Cup.

Nick Skelton, three times King's winner (1984, 1993 and 1999), came up with what seems to me like a good compromise idea. He suggested that the highest-placed woman in the King George should receive the Queen's Cup. He welcomed the idea of there being only the one Grand Prix, because it would mean more prize money, but added that he thought the Hickstead Derby, which has the biggest cash prize in Britain, should be brought into this show, instead of its month-earlier slot, because that would result in more international riders participating.

The change apparently came as a result of an FEI view that having classes segregated by sex was contrary to the way they like to do things. They were particularly concerned that the prize money for the men's class was three times that for the women's.

The prize money for the King George V Gold Cup was increased to £60,000, up from £45,000 the previous year, with £20,000 of the prize fund going to the winner.

No less illustrious than the men's King George is the roll call of past Queen Elizabeth winners, including Marion Mould (*née* Coakes), three times, twice with Stroller and in 1976 with Elizabeth Ann; Pat Smythe,

DID YOU KNOW?

Before the 1984 Olympic Games, HRH Prince Philip, the Duke of Edinburgh, who was president of the International Equestrian Federation, warned all the National Federations that if they did not 'put their house in order' in terms of which riders were professionals and which were amateurs (which Olympic athletes were, in those days, supposed to be) equestrian sport might be excluded from the Olympic Games.

The British Federation did so, expecting other Federations to follow suit, but none did. It meant that, with the likes of Harvey Smith and David Broome barred from representing their country, a youthful and comparatively inexperienced team had to be chosen.

The quartet of John and Michael Whitaker, Tim Grubb and Harvey's son Steven Smith performed mightily to gain a silver medal behind the USA. Michael Whitaker had one of only two clears in the first round on Overton Amanda, but missed out on an individual medal in the second round.

The ban on professionals was lifted in 1987 with the introduction of 'Competitor Status'.

Caroline Bradley and, for Ireland, Jessica Kurten. Liz Edgar won it a remarkable five times on three different horses, culminating with Rapier in 1986. The last holder of the women-only Queen's Cup was Tina Fletcher, who in 2007 won the trophy for the third time; her prize was £6,000.

THE AGA KHAN CUP, IRELAND

The highlight of the Dublin Horse Show each August is the Aga Khan Cup, which came about after Colonel Zeigler of the Swiss Army suggested holding an international jumping event there. The Aga Khan of the time, 1925, heard of this proposal and offered a magnificent challenge trophy to the winner of the competition, in appreciation of all the pleasures he had had at previous horse shows and in gratitude of his Irish tutor, Mr Kenny.

The Aga Khan Cup is Ireland's Nations Cup competition and is held on the Friday of the five-day show. Six countries competed that first year, 1926: Great Britain, Holland, Belgium, France, Switzerland and Ireland. The Swiss team won the title on Irish-bred horses. The Swiss won again the next year but in 1928 the Irish team of Captains Dan Corry, Jed O'Dwyer and Cyril Harty lifted the trophy.

The original trophy was won outright by the Swiss in 1930. After that, it could only be retained if won three times in succession. Ireland won the first replacement in 1937, amid great excitement. The outcome depended on the last Irish horse to achieve a clear round; Red Hugh, ridden by Captain Dan Corry, was foot-perfect and the trophy was Ireland's to keep. The winning team was Commandant J.G. O'Dwyer on Clontarf, Captain J.J. Lewis on Glendalough and Captain D. Corry on Red Hugh. Incredibly, Ireland won it again the next year, which makes four in a row. Captain Dan Corry was in the winning team a total of seven times and Jed O'Dwyer six times. This meant that 1938 saw the third trophy donated by the Aga Khan.

The United States became the first non-European winners in 1948. This was the year when, for the first time, each country was represented by a team of four horses, with the best three counting at the finish, a format that has continued ever since. There was another change in 1951 when, following the start of speed competitions on the Continent, the clock came into play for the first time when a time limit was introduced.

Britain won the trophy outright in 1953. There was no competition in 1952 because of the Olympic Games in Helsinki, but Colonel Harry Llewellyn and Foxhunter and Peter Robeson on Craven A were in the winning teams of 1950, '51 and '53; Britain made it four in a row in 1954. In 1953, instead of each team jumping as a unit (which could mean the result of the competition was known well before the end), the present-day system was introduced, whereby the first rider of each country jumps, followed by the second rider of each country, and the third and the fourth. This adds greatly to the anticipation and excitement.

It was not until 1954 that women were allowed to ride for their countries, (now an international rule). This year also saw the fourth Aga Khan Trophy, a magnificent gold cup of Georgian-period design, standing on an ebony plinth 2ft 3in high.

In 1966 an outbreak of swamp fever in Europe resulted in a ban on Continental horses entering Britain or Ireland, which meant there could be no Aga Khan Trophy as such that year. Instead, a competition was organised between two British teams and two Irish teams, one army and one civilian. It was the only occasion when two such Irish teams competed against each other. The British 'B' team won.

Britain won the trophy outright again in 1975. David Broome was in all three winning teams of 1973 to 1975, as well as that of 1970. The later 1970s belonged to Ireland, who won the trophy outright for a second time in 1979. The quartet of Paul Darragh, Captain Con Power, James Kernan and Eddie Macken were the riders in all these victories from 1976 to 1979.

In both 1978 and '79 the result had to be decided after a jump-off against Britain. The present trophy is the sixth in the series and was presented by His Highness the Aga Khan in 1980.

Ireland and Great Britain were to dominate the next couple of decades; other nations to win were the USA, Germany and Switzerland during the 1980s; the USA again in 1993, and Italy and the Netherlands at the end of that decade.

There was a broader mix in the new millennium, with Belgium, France twice, Germany twice, the Netherlands and Italy all getting their names inscribed on the trophy, along with Britain and Ireland.

HORSE HUMOUR

You know you're a horse person when ... every time you drive past a road-construction sight you think what nice jumps the barricades would make.

In 2014 the USA won with a team including Jessica Springsteen riding Vindicat, who for Peter Charles had been part of the British gold-medal winning Olympic team in London 2012. Jessica's father, singer Bruce Springsteen, more used to taking centre stage in the RDS Arena, was among the audience.

The 2015 Aga Khan Cup in Dublin produced a convincing win for the home team. The Irish were so far ahead of their rivals that their last horse did not have to jump in the final round. It also saw the one hundredth cap for Irish rider Cian O'Connor. The winning team was Bertram Allen on Romanov, Greg Broderick on MHS Going Global, Darragh Kenny on Sans Souci Z and Cian O'Connor on Good Luck.

The Puissance competition, with a prize fund of €30,000 making it the richest in the world, was won by Northern Ireland-based Egyptian rider Sameh El Dahan. He took the €12,400 winner's purse on the fourth jump-off, riding an Irish Sport Horse, Britt Megahey's gelding Seapatrick Cruise Cavalier.

Sunday's culmination, the €200,000 Grand Prix, was won by Kent Farrington of the USA ahead of Ireland's US-based Kevin Babbington, with Conor Swail in third.

9

RESULTS, RECORDS AND STATISTICS

BSJA CHAIRMEN AND PRESIDENTS

Chairmen
1945-1956 Lieutenant-Colonel C.T. Walwyn, DSO, OBE, MC
1957-9 His Grace the Duke of Norfolk, KG, PC, GCVO
1959-60 His Grace The Duke of Northumberland, KG, MFH
1962 His Grace The Duke of Beaufort
1963 HRH The Princess Royal, CI, CVO, GBE
1964-6 Lieutenant-Colonel M. Ansell CBE, DSO
1967-8 Colonel W.H. Whitbread, TD
1969-70 Lieutenant-Colonel Lord Leigh, TD
1971 The Earl of Westmorland, KCVO
1972-4 Lord Rupert Neville, JP, DL
1975-6 Lieutenant-Colonel H.M. Llewellyn, CBE
1977-9 Gen. Sir Cecil Blacker, GCB, OBE, MC
1980–3 Mr A.J. Blakeway
1984–1990 Colonel P. Drew
1991–2 Mr Michael Bates
1993–5 Mr Douglas Bunn
1996–7 Mr David Broome, CBE
1998–9 Mr Phillip Billington
2001–2 Mr Peter Gillespie
2003–4 Mr John Jacks
2005–13 Mr Michael Mac
2013–Mr Les Harris and Mr Michael Mac
2014–5 (on-going) Mr Les Harris

Presidents
1980 General Sir Cecil Blacker, GCB, OBE, MC
1981–3 His Grace the Duke of Wellington
1984–86-Mrs P. Koechlin-Smythe, OBE

1987 R. Dean, CBE
1988 –
1989–93 Lieutenant-Colonel Sir John Miller, GCVO, DSO, MC
1994–97 Lord King of Wartnaby
1998–2000 Colonel Phillip R. Drew, OBE, TD
1999–2002 Douglas Bunn
2001–4 John Hales
2009–12 Elizabeth Astall
2013–15 (on-going) David Broome, CBE

OLYMPIC GAMES 1900, PARIS

'Prize jumping' for high jump and long jump became an equestrian discipline at the 1900 Olympic Games in Paris, the second games of the modern Olympiad and the first in which women were allowed to compete, but it was not until the 1912 Stockholm Olympics that a Nations Cup-style show-jumping event was staged. The Paris results were as follows:

Prize Jumping
Gold: Aime Haegeman, Benton 11, Belgium
Silver: Georges van de Poele, Squire, Belgium
Bronze: Louis de Champsavin, Gerpsichore, France

Long Jump
Gold: Constant van Langendonck, Extra Dry, Belgium, 6.10m
Silver: Gian Giorgio Trissino, Oreste, Italy, 5.70m
Bronze: Lt de Bellegarde, Tolla, France, 5.30m

High Jump
Gold: Dominique Maximien Garderes, Canela, France, 1.85m
Silver: Gian Giorgio Trissino, Oreste, Italy, 1.85m
Bronze: Georges van de Poele, Ludlow, Belgium 1.70m

OLYMPIC GAMES INDIVIDUAL RESULTS

	Gold	Silver	Bronze
1912 Stockholm			
Rider	Jean Cariou	Rabod von Kröcher	Emmanuel de Blommaert

Horse	Mignon	Dohna	Clonmore
Nation	France	Germany	Belgium
1920 Antwerp			
Rider	Tommaso Lequio di Assaba	Alessandro Valerio	Carl Gustaf Lewenhaupt
Horse	Trebecco	Cento	Mon Coeur
Nation	Italy	Italy	Sweden
1924 Paris			
Rider	Alphonse Gemuseus	Tommaso Lequio di Assaba	Adam Królikiewicz
Horse	Lucette	Trebecco	Picador
Nation	Switzerland	Italy	Poland
1928 Amsterdam			
Rider	Fratišek Ventura	Pierre Bertran de Balanda	Charles-Gustave Kuhn
Horse	Elliot	Papillion	Pepita
Nation	Czechoslovakia	France	Switzerland
1932 Los Angeles			
Rider	Takeichi Nishi	Harry Chamberlin	Clarence von Rosen, Jr
Horse	Uranus	Show Girl	Empire
Nation	Japan	USA	Sweden
1936 Berlin			
Rider	Kurt Hasse	Henri Rang	József von Platthy
Horse	Tora	Delfis	Sello
Nation	Germany	Romania	Hungary
1948 London			
Rider	Humberto Mariles	Rubén Uriza	Jean-François d'Orgeix
Horse	Arete	Harvey	Sucre de Pomme
Nation	Mexico	Mexico	France
1952 Helsinki			
Rider	Pierre Jonquères d'Oriola	Oscar Cristi	Fritz Thiedermann

Horse	Ali Baba	Bambi	Meteor
Nation	France	Chile	West Germany
1956 Stockholm			
Rider	Han Günter Winkler	Raimondo D'Inzeo	Piero D'Inzeo
Horse	Halla	Merano	Uruguay
Nation	West Germany	Italy	Italy
1960 Rome			
Rider	Raimondo D'Inzeo	Piero D'Inzeo	David Broome
Horse	Posillipo	The Rock	Sunsalve
Nation	Italy	Italy	Great Britain
1964 Tokyo			
Rider	Pierre Jonquères d'Oriola	Hermann Schridde	Peter Robeson
Horse	Lutteur	Dozent	Firecrest
Nation	France	West Germany	Great Britain
1968 Mexico City			
Rider	William Steinkraus	Marion Coakes	David Broome
Horse	Snowbound	Stroller	Mister Softee
Nation	USA	Great Britain	Great Britain
1972 Munich			
Rider	Graziano Mancinelli	Ann Moore	Neal Shaprio
Horse	Ambassador	Psalm	Sloopy
Nation	Italy	Great Britain	USA
1976 Montreal			
Rider	Alwin Schockemöhle	Michel Vaillancourt	Francois Mathy
Horse	Warwick Rex	Branch County	Gai Luron
Nation	West Germany	Canada	Belgium
1980 Moscow			
Rider	Jan Kowalczyk	Nikolai Koroilkov	Joaquin Perez Heras

Horse	Artemor	Espadron	Alymony
Nation	Poland	Soviet Union	Mexico
1984 Los Angeles			
Rider	Joseph Fargis	Conrad Homfeld	Heidi Robbiani
Horse	Touch of Class	Abdullah	Jessica V
Nation	USA	USA	Switzerland
1988 Seoul			
Rider	Pierre Durand, Jr	Greg Best	Karsten Huck
Horse	Jappeloup	Gem Twist	Nepomuk
Nation	France	USA	West Germany
1992 Barcelona			
Rider	Ludger Beerbaum	Piet Raymakers	Norman Dello Joio
Horse	Classic Touch	Ratina Z	Irish
Nation	Germany	Netherlands	USA
1996 Atlanta			
Rider	Ulrich Kirchhoff	Willi Melliger	Alexandra Ledermann
Horse	Jus de Pommes	Calvaro	Rochet M
Nation	Germany	Switzerland	France
2000 Sydney			
Rider	Jeroen Dubbeldam	Albert Voorn	Khaled Al-Eid
Horse	De Sjiem	Lando	Khashm Al Aan
Nation	Netherlands	Netherlands	Saudi Arabia
2004 Athens			
Rider	Rodrigo Pessoa	Chris Kappler	Marco Kutsher
Horse	Baloubet du Rouet	Royal Kaliber	Montender 2
Nation	Brazil	USA	Germany
2008 Beijing			
Rider	Eric Lamaze	Rolf-Göran Bengtsson	Beezie Madden
Horse	Hickstead	Ninja	Authentic

DID YOU KNOW?

When Graziano Mancinelli won the individual gold medal for Italy in the 1972 Olympics in Munich, journalists were told at the post-event press conference that 'Mancinelli had nothing to say to the Press'. Eventually he arrived but did indeed have little to say.

However, the British Press were fully engaged with talking to silver-medal winner, Ann Moore.

Riding the small bay Psalm, the horse jumped so high at the second fence of the second round that Ann lost both her stirrup irons and jumped the next fence, a huge double of oxers, without them – but knocked both elements. Nevertheless, she was through to the timed jump-off and, attempting to cut seconds off Graziano Mancinelli's clear round, she turned too sharply at the second, causing Psalm to refuse; they had no further faults and finished with a silver medal.

Nation	Canada	Sweden	USA
2012 London			
Rider	Steve Guerdat	Gerco Schroder	Cian O'Connor
Horse	Nino De Buissonets	London	Blue Loyd 12
Nation	Switzerland	Netherlands	Ireland

OLYMPIC GAMES TEAM RESULTS

	Gold	Silver	Bronze
1912 Stockholm			
Riders	Gustaf Lewenhaupt, Gustaf Kilman, Hans von Rosen, Fredrik Rosencrantz	Michel Dufourt, Jean Cariou, Ernest Meyer and Gaston Seigner	Sigismund Freyer, Wilhelm von Hohenau, Ernst Deloch and Prince Friedrich Karl of Prussia

Horses	Medusa, Gátan, Lord Iron, Drabant	Amazone Mignon, Allons-y, Cocotte	Ultimus, Pretty Girl, Hubertus, Gibson Boy
Nation	Sweden	France	Germany
1920 Antwerp			
Riders	Claës König, Hans von Rosen, Daniel Norling, Frank Martin	Henri Laame, André Coumans, Herman de Gaiffier d'Hestroy, Herman d'Oultromont	Ettore Caffaratti, Alessandro Alvisi, Giulio Cacciandra, Carlo Asinari
Horses	Tresor, Poor Boy, Eros, Kohort	Biscuit, Lisette, Miss, Lord Kitchener	Tradittore, Raggio di Sole, Fortunello, Varone
Nation	Sweden	Belgium	Italy
1924 Paris			
Riders	Åke Thelning, Axel Ståhle, Åge Lundström	Alphonse Gemuseus, Werner Stuber, Hans Bühler	António Borges, Hélder de Souza, José Mouzinho
Horses	Loke, Cecil, Anvers	Lucette, Girandole, Sailor Boy	Reginald, Avro, Hetrugo
Nation	Sweden	Switzerland	Portugal
1928 Amsterdam			
Riders	José Navarro Morenes, José Álvarez de Bohórquez, Julio García Fernándex de Ios Ríos	Kazimierz Gzowski, Kazimierz Szosland, Michał Antoniewicz	Karl Hansén, Björnstjerna, Ernst Hallberg
Horses	Zapatazo, Zalamero, Revistade	Mylord, Ali, Readgleadt	Gerold, Kornett, Loke
Nation	Spain	Poland	Sweden

1932 Los Angeles – no team competition			
1936 Berlin			
Riders	Kurt Hasse, Marten von Barnekow, Heinz Brandt	Johan Greter, Jan de Bruine, Henri van Schaik	José Belträo, Domingos de Sousa, Luís Mena e Silva
Horses	Tora, Nordland, Alchimist	Ernica, Trixie, Santa Bell	Biscuit, Merle Blanc, Fossette
Nation	Germany	Netherlands	Portugal
1948 London			
Riders	Humberto Mariles, Rubén Uriza, Alberto Valdés	Jaime García, José Navarro Morenes, Gavilán	Harry Llewellyn, Henry Nicoll, Arthur Carr
Horses	Arete, Harvey, ChihuchocP	Bizarro, Quórum, Forajido	Foxhunter, Kilgeddin, Monty
Nation	Mexico	Spain	Great Britain
1952 Helsinki			
Riders	Wilfred White, Douglas Stewart, Harry Llewellyn	Óscar Cristi, César Mendoza, Ricardo Echeverría	William Steinkraus, Arthus McCashin, John William Russell
Horses	Nizefela, Aherlow, Foxhunter	Bambi, Pillán, Lindo Peal	Hollandia, Miss Budweiser, Democrat
Nation	Great Britain	Chile	USA
1956 Stockholm			
Riders	Hans Günter Winkler, Fritz Thiedemann, Alfons Lütke-Westhues	Raimondo D'Inzeo, Piero D'Inzeo, Salvatore Oppes	Wilfred White, Pat Smythe, Peter Robeson
Horses	Halla, Meteor, Ala	Merano, Uruguay, Pagoro	Nizefela, Flanagan, Scorchin
Nation	Germany	Italy	Great Britain

1960 Rome			
Riders	Hans Günter Winkler, Thiedemann Alwin Schockemöhle	Frank Chapot, William Steinkraus, George Morris	Raimondo D'Inzeo, Piero D'Inzeo, Antonio Oppes
Horses	Halla, Meteor, Ferdl	Trail Guide, Ksar d'Esprit, Sinjon	Posillipo, The Rock, The Scholar
Nation	Germany	USA	Italy
1964 Tokyo			
Riders	Hermann Schridde, Kurt Jarasinski, Hans Günter Winkler	Pierre Jonquères d'Oriola, Janou Lefèbvre, Guy Lefrant	Piero D'Inzeo, Raimondo D'Inzeo, Graziano Mancinelli
Horses	Dozent II, Torro, Fidelitas	Lutteur B, Kenavo D, Monsieur de Littry	Sun Beam, Posillipo, Rockette
Nation	Germany	France	Italy
1968 Mexico City			
Riders	James Day, Thomas Gayford, Jim Elder	Jean Rozier, Janou Lefèbvre, Pierre Jonquères d'Oriola	Hermann Schridde, Alwin Schockemöhle, Hans Günter Winkler
Horses	Canadian Club, Big Dee, The Immigrant	Quo Vadis, Rocket, Nagir	Dozent II, Donald Rex, Enigk
Nation	Canada	France	West Germany
1972 Munich			
Riders	Fritz Ligges, Gerhard Wiltfang, Hartwig Steenken, Hans Günter Winkler	William Steinkraus, Neal Shapiro, Kathryn Kusner, Frank Chapot	Vittorio Orlandi, Raimondo D'Inzeo, Graziano Mancinelli, Piero D'Inzeo
Horses	Robin, Askan, Simona, Trophy	Main Spring, Sloopy, Fleet Apple, White Lightning	Fulmer Feather, Fiorello, Ambassador, Easter Light

Nation	West Germany	USA	Italy
1976 Montreal			
Riders	Hubert Parot, Jean-Marcel Rozier, Marc Roquet, Michel Roche	Alwin Schockemöhle, Hans Günter Winkler, Sönke Sönksen, Paul Schockemöhle	Eric Wauters, François Mathy, Edgar-Henri Cuepper, Stanny Van Paesschen
Horses	Rivage, Bayard de Maupas, Belle de Mars, Un Espoir	Warwick Rex, Trophy, Kwepe, Agent	Gute Sitte, Gai Luron, Le Champion, Porsche
Nation	France	West Germany	Belgium
1980 Moscow			
Riders	Vyacgeslav Chukanov, Viktor Poganovsky, Viktor Asmaev, Nikolai Korolkov	Marian Kozicki, Jan Kowalczyk, Wiesław Hartman, Janusz Bobik	Joaquin Perez Heras, Jesus Gomez Portugal, Valencia Gerardo Tazzer, Alberto Valdes Lacarra
Horses	Gepatit, Toky, Reis, Espadron	Bremen, Artemor, Norton, Szampan	Alymony, Massacre, Caribe, Lady Mirka
Nation	Soviet Union	Poland	Mexico
1984 Los Angeles			
Riders	Joseph Fargis, Conrad Homfeld, Leslie Howard, Melanie Smith	Michael Whitaker, John Whitaker, Steven Smith, Timothy Grubb	Paul Schockemöhle, Peter Luther, Franke Sloothaak, Fritz Ligges
Horses	Touch of Class, Abdullah, Albany, Calypso	Overton Amanda, Ryan's Son, Shining Example, Linky	Deister, Livius, Farmer, Ramzes
Nation	USA	Great Britain	West Germany

1988 Seoul			
Riders	Ludger Beerbaum, Wolfgang Brinkmann, Dirk Hafemeister, Franke Sloothaak	Gred Best, Lisa Ann Jacquin, Anne Kursinski, Joseph Fargis	Hubert Bourdy, Frédèric Cottier, Michel Robert, Pierre Durand, Jr
Horses	The Freak, Pedro, Orchidee 76, Walzerkonig 19	Gem Twist, For the Moment, Starman, Mill Pearl	Morgat, Flambeau C, La Fayette, Jappeloup de Luze
Nation	West Germany	USA	France
1992 Barcelona			
Riders	Piet Raymakers, Bert Romp, Jan Tops, Jos Lansink	Boris Boor, Joerg Muenzner, Hugo Simon, Thomas Fruehmann	Hervé Godignon, Hubert Bourdy, Michel Robert, Eric Navet
Horses	Ratina Z, Waldo E, Top Gun, Egano	Love Me Tender, Graf Grande, Apricot D, Genius	Quidam de Revel, Razzina du Poncel, Nonix, Quito de Baussy
Nation	Netherlands	Austria	France
1996 Atlanta			
Riders	Franke Sloothaak, Lars Nieberg, Ulrich Kirchhoff, Ludger Beerbaum	Peter Leone, Leslie, Burre-Howard, Anne Kursinski, Michael Matz	Luiz Felipe De Azevedo, Álvaro Miranda Neto, André Johannpeter, Rodrigo Pessoa
Horses	Joly Coeur, For Pleasure, Jus De Pommes, Ratina Z	Legato, Extreme, Eros, Rhum	Cassiana, Aspen, Calei, Tomboy
Nation	Germany	USA	Brazil
2000 Sydney			
Riders	Ludger Beerbaum, Lars Nieberg, Marcus Ehning, Otto Becker	Markus Fuchs, Beat Maendli, Lesley McNaught, Willi Melliger	Rodrigo Pessoa, Luiz Felipe De Azevedo, Álvaro Miranda Neto, André Johannpeter

Horses	Goldfever 3 Wsprit FRH, For Pleasure, Dobels Cento	Tinka's Boy, Pozitano, Dulf, Calvaro V	Baloubet du Rouet, Ralph, Aspen, Calei
Nation	Germany	Switzerland	Brazil
2004 Athens			
Riders	Peter Wylde, McLain Ward, Beezie Madden, Chris Kappler	Rolf-Göran Bengtsson, Malin Baryard, Peter Eriksson, Peder Fredericson	Otto Becker, Maro Kutscher, Christian Ahlmann
Horses	Fein Cera, Sapphire, Authentic, Royal Kaliber	Mac Kinley, Butterfly Flip, Cardento, Magic Bengtsson	Dobels Cento, Montender 2, Cöster
Nation	USA	Sweden	Germany
2008 Beijing			
Riders	McLain Ward, Laura Kraut, Will Simpson, Beezie Madden	Jill Henselwood, Eric Lamaze, Ian Millar, Mac Cone	Christina Liebherr, Pius Schwizer, Niklaus Schurtenberger, Steve Guerdat
Horses	Sapphire, Cedric, Carlsson vom Dach, Authentic	Special Ed, Hickstead, In Style, Ole	No Mercy, Nobless M, Cantus, Jalisca Solier
Nation	USA	Canada	Switzerland
2012 London			
Riders	Scott Brash, Peter Charles, Ben Maher, Nick Skelton	Marc Houtzager, Gerco Schroder, Maikel van der Vleuten, Jur Vrieling	Ramzy Al Duhami, HRH Prince Abdullah Al Saud, Kamal Bahamdan, Abdullah Waleed Sharbatly
Horses	Hello Sanctos, Vindicat, Tripple X, Big Star	Tamino, London, Verdi, Bubalu	Bayard Van the Villa There, Davos, Noblesse Des Tess, Sultan
Nation	Great Britain	Netherlands	Saudi Arabia

KING GEORGE V GOLD CUP WINNERS

Date	Horse	Rider	Country
1911	Piccolo	Dimitri d'Exe	Russia
1912	Murat	Lt Delvoie	Belgium
1913	Amazone	Baron de Maelon	France
1914	Amazone	Baron de Maelon	France
1915	-	-	-
1916	-	-	-
1917	-	-	-
1918	-	-	-
1919	-	-	-
1920	Dignite	Auguste de Laissardiere	France
1921	Combined Training	Geoffrey Brooke	Great Britain
1922	Bluff	Conte Giacomo Antonelli	Italy
1923	Grey Fox	Auguste de Laissardiere	France
1924	Don Chisciotte	Coonte Giulio Borsaelli di Riffredo	Italy
1925	Broncho	Malise Graham	Great Britain
1926	Ballymacshane	Fred Bontecou	USA
1927	Quinine	Xavier Bizard	France
1928	Forty Six	A.G. Martyr	Great Britain
1929	Mandarin	Hubert Gibault	France
1930	Chelsea	Jack Talbot-Ponsonby	Great Britain
1931	The Parson	Jacques Misonne	Belgium
1932	Chelsea	Jack Talbot-Ponsonby	Great Britain
1933	Best Girl	Jack Talbot-Ponsonby	Great Britain
1934	Tramore Bay	John Lewis	Ireland
1935	Limerick Lace	Jed O'Dwyer	Ireland

1936	-	-	-
1937	Honduras	Xavier Bizard	France
1938	Derek	John Friedberger	Great Britain
1939	Adigrat	Conte Alessandro Bettoni-Cazzago	Italy
1940	-	-	-
1941	-	-	-
1942	-	-	-
1943	-	-	-
1944	-	-	-
1945	-	-	-
1946	-	-	-
1947	Marquis III	Pierre Jonquerer d'Oriola	France
1948	Foxhunter	Harry Llewellyn	Great Britain
1949	Tankard	Brian Butler	Great Britain
1950	Foxhunter	Harry Llewellyn	Great Britain
1951	Ballyneety	Kevin Barry	Ireland
1952	Grecieux	Carlos Figueroa	Spain
1953	Foxhunter	Harry Llewellyn	Great Britain
1954	Meteor	Fritz Thiedemann	Germany
1955	Brando	Luigi Cartasegna	Italy
1956	First Boy	William Steinkraus	USA
1957	Uruguay	Piero d'Inzeo	Italy
1958	Master William	Hugh Wiley	USA
1959	Nautical	Hugh Wiley	USA
1960	Sunsalve	David Broome	Great Britain
1961	The Rock	Piero d'Inzeo	Italy
1962	The Rock	Piero d'Inzeo	Italy
1963	Dundrum	Tommy Wade	Ireland
1964	Sinjon	William Steinkraus	USA
1965	Fortun	Hans Günter Winkler	Germany
1966	Mister Softee	David Broome	Great Britain
1967	Firecrest	Peter Robeson	Great Britain

1968	Enigk	Hans Günter Winkler	Great Britain
1969	Uncle Max	Ted Edgar	Great Britain
1970	Mattie Brown	Harvey Smith	Great Britain
1971	Askan	Gerd Wiltfang	Germany
1972	Sportsman	David Broome	Great Britain
1973	Pennwood Forge Mill	Paddy McMahon	Great Britain
1974	Mainspring	Frank Chapot	USA
1975	Rex the Robber	Alvin Schockemöhle	Germany
1976	Chainbridge	Mike Saywell	Great Britain
1977	Philco	David Broome	Great Britain
1978	Claret	Jeff McVean	Austria
1979	Video	Robert Smith	Great Britain
1980	Scorton	David Bowen	Great Britain
1981	Mr Ross	David Broome	Great Britain
1982	Disney Way	Michael Whitaker	Great Britain
1983	Deister	Paul Schockemöhle	Germany
1984	St James	Nick Skelton	Great Britain
1985	Towerlands Anglezarke	Malcolm Pyrah	Great Britain
1986	Next Ryan's Son	John Whitaker	Great Britain
1987	Towerlands Anglezarke	Malcom Pyrah	Great Britain
1988	Brook St Boysie	Robert Smith	Great Britain
1989	Next Didi	Michael Whitaker	Great Britain
1990	Henderson Milton	John Whitaker	Great Britain
1991	Lannegan	David Broome	Great Britain
1992	Everest Midnight Madness	Michael Whitaker	Great Britain
1993	Everest Limited Edition	Nick Skelton	Great Britain
1994	Everest Midnight Magic	Michael Whitaker	Great Britain
1995	Heather Blaze	Robert Splaine	Ireland

1996	Cathleen	Nick Skelton	Great Britain
1997	Virtual Village Welham	John Whitaker	Great Britain
1998	Senator Mighty Blue	Robert Smith	Great Britain
1999	Hopes are High	Nick Skelton	Great Britain
2000	Ballaseyr Twilight	Cameron Hanley	Ireland
2001	Glasgow	Norman Dello Joio	USA
2002	Champion du Lys	Ludger Beerbaum	Germany
2003	Carling King	Keving Babington	Ireland
2004	Farina	Rene Tebbel	Germany
2005	Armani	Jeffrey Welles	USA
2006	Ideal de la Loge	Roger-Yves Bost	France
2007	Jubilee D'Ouilly	Aymeric de Ponnat	France
2008	Clausen	Holger Wulschner	Germany
2009	Murka's Pall Mall H	Peter Charles	Great Britain
2010	Fresh Direct Kalico Bay	Tim Stockdale	Great Britain
2011	Uceko	Kent Farrington	USA
2012	Cerona	Hendrik-Jan Schuttert	Netherlands
2013	Tripple X III	Ben Maher	Great Britain
2014	Cortes 'C'	Beezie Madden	USA
2015	Cortes 'C'	Beezie Madden	USA

DID YOU KNOW?

Great crested newts like to set up home in the water jump at Hickstead and the local amphibian society has to come every year to take them away.

The World Individual Championships was opened to women along with the men in 1978, the year which saw a Team Championship in addition to the Individual. Before that there had been three Women's World Championships, in 1965, 1970 and 1974. Men had had an Individual Championship since 1953.

NATIONS CUP AGA KHAN CUP WINNERS

1926 Switzerland			
Riders	Capt. von der Weid	Capt. H Bühler	Maj. C. Kuhn	-
Horses	Royal Gris	Vladimir	Novello	-
1927 Switzerland			
Riders	Capt. von der Weid	Capt. Hersche	Lt Gemuseus	-
Horses	Royal Gris	Esperance	Notas	-
1928 Ireland			
Riders	Capt. Dan Corry	Capt. Ged O'Dwyer	Capt. Cyril Harty	-
Horses	Finglin	Cuchulain	Craobh Ruadh	-
1929 France			
Riders	Lt Clavé	Lt de Rolland	Lt Bizard	-
Horses	Volant III	Scouissant III	Perigord	-
1930 Switzerland			
Riders	Lt F.B. Daetwiler	Maj. C. Kuhn	Lt O.K. Degallier	-

Horses	Turgi	Corona	Notas	-
1931 Great Britain				
Riders	Maj. Joseph Hume Dudgeon	Capt. W.H. Muir	Lt J.A. Talbot-Ponsonby	-
Horses	Standard	Seacount	Irish Eagle	-
1932 Ireland				
Riders	Capt. Ged O'Dwyer	Capt. Dan Leonard	Capt. Fred Aherne	-
Horses	Limerick Lace	Miss Ireland	Ireland's Own	-
1933 France				
Riders	Capt. H. du Breuil	Lt P. Cavaillé	Lt T. de Tiliere	-
Horses	Exercise	Olivette	Papillon XlV	-
1934 Germany				
Riders	Rittmeister Von Salviata	Ober Lt Shilicum	Rittmeister Von Barnekon	-
Horses	Senator	Dedo	Nicoline	-
1935 Ireland				
Riders	Comdt Ged O'Dwyer	Capt. Fred Aherne	Capt. Dan Corry	-
Horses	Limerick Lace	Blarney Castle	Miss Ireland	-
1936 Ireland				
Riders	Comdt Ged O'Dwyer	Capt. Jack Lewis	Capt. Dan Corry	-
Horses	Clontarf	Glendalough	Red Hugh	-
1938 Ireland				
Riders	Capt. Fred Aherne	Capt. Dan Corry	Comdt. Ged O'Dwyer	-
Horses	Duhallow	Red Hugh	Limerick Lace	-
1938 Ireland				
Riders	Capt. Fred Aherne	Capt. Dan Corry	Comdt. Ged O'Dwyer	-
Horses	Blarney Castle	Duhallow	Limerick Lace	-
1939 France				
Riders	Capt. J. Chevallier	Lt M. Fresson	Lt de Bartillat	-

Horses	Jacynthe	Homlette	Cambrome	-
1940-1945 No competition				
1946 Ireland				
Riders	Comdt Dan Corry	Capt. Jack Stack	Lt Col. Jack lewis	-
Horses	Antrim Glens	Tramore Bay	Clontibret	-
1947 Great Britain				
Riders	Maj. A. Carr	Lt Col. H.M. Nicholl	Lt Col. A.B. Scott	-
Horses	Notar	Pepper Pot	Lucky Dip	-
1948 USA				
Riders	Capt. J.W. Russell	Col. F.F. Wing	Lt Col. C. Anderson	Lt Col. C. Symroski
Horses	Airmail	Democrat	Riem	Nipper
1949 Ireland				
Riders	Lt Col. D. Corry	Capt. W.B. Mullins	Capt. M. Tubridy	Capt. O'Shea
Horses	Clonakilty	Bruree	Lough Neagh	Rostrevor
1950 Great Britain				
Riders	Lt Col. H.M. Nicholl	Lt Col. H.M. Llewellyn	Lt M. Webber	Mr Peter Robeson
Horses	Pepper Pot	Foxhunter	Nightbird	Craven 'A'
1951 Great Britain				
Riders	A. Massarella	Peter Robeson	E. Holland-Martin	Lt Col. H.M. Llewellyn
Horses	The Monarch	Craven 'A'	Aherlow	Foxhunter
1952 No competition				
1953 Great Britain				
Riders	Peter Robeson	W.R. Hanson	Capt. W.H. White	Lt Col. H. Llewellyn
Horses	Craven 'A'	The Monarch	Nizafela	Foxhunter
1954 Great Britain				
Riders	Lt Col. H.M. Nicholl	Donald Beard	Lt Col. D.N. Stewart	Peter Robeson
Horses	Pepper Pot	Costa	The Monarch	Craven 'A'

1955 Italy				
Riders	Capt. S. Oppes	Lt Col. L. Cartasegne	Lt Raimondo d'Inzeo	Capt. S. Oppes
Horses	Pagora	Brando	Merano	The Quiet Man
1956 Great Britain				
Riders	Dawn Palet	John Lanni	Mary Marshall	Lt Col. H.M. Llewellyn
Horses	Earlsrath Rambler	Huntsman Six	Nobbler	Aherlow
1957 France				
Riders	Capt. Lefrant	Capt. de Fombelle	Jean d'Orgieux	Capt. de Fombelle
Horses	Caballero II	Grand Veneur	Topinambur	Bucephale
1958 Great Britain				
Riders	Jill Banks	George Hobbs	T.M. Charlesworth	Harvey Smith
Horses	Earlsrath Rambler	Royal Lord	Smokey Bob	Farmers Boy
1959 Great Britain				
Riders	Jill Banks	Dawn Wofford	Susan Cohen	Douglas Bunn
Horses	Earlsrath Rambler	Hollandia	Clare Castle	Coady
1960 Argentina				
Riders	Lt Col. C. Delia	Lt Naldo Dasso	Jorge Lucardi	Ernest Hartkopf
Horses	Huipil	Final	Stromboli	Baltasar
1961 Germany				
Riders	Thomas Bagusat	Hermann Schridde	Alwin Schockemöhle	Hans Gunther Winkler
Horses	Bajazzo 3	Fugosa	Ferdl	Feuerdorn
1962 Italy				
Riders	Capt. Piero d'Inzeo	G. Mancinelli	Dr Ugo d'Amelio	Capt. Raimondo d'Inzeo
Horses	The Rock	Rockette	Fancy Socks	Posillipo

1963 Ireland				
Riders	Tommy Wade	Capt. Bill Ringrose	Hon. Diana Conolly-Carew	Seamus Hayes
Horses	Dundrum	Loch an Easpaig	Barrymore	Goodbye
1964 USA				
Riders	Mary Mairs	Kathy Kusner	Frank Chapot	William Steinkraus
Horses	Tomboy	Untouchable	Manon	Sinjon
1965 Great Britain				
Riders	Harvey Smith	David Barker	Marion Coakes	Valery Barker
Horses	Harvester VI	O'Malley	Stroller	Atalanta
1966 No competition				
1967 Ireland				
Riders	Seamus Hayes	Capt. Ned Campion	Tommy Wade	Comdt Bill Ringrose
Horses	Goodbye	Liathdruim	Dundrum	Loch an Easpaig
1968 USA				
Riders	Mary Chapot	Kathy Kusner	Frank Chapot	William Steinkraus
Horses	White Lightning	Fru	San Lucas	Snowbound
1969 Germany				
Riders	Lutz Merkel	Hartwig Steenken	Hans Gunther Winkler	Paul Schockemöhle
Horses	Sir	Simone	Torphy	Donald
1970 Great Britain				
Riders	Michael Saywell	Harvey Smith	George Hobbs	David Broome
Horses	Hideaway	Mattie Brown	Battling Pedulas	Manhattan
1971 Germany				
Riders	Hendrik Snoek	Gerd Wiltfang	Hans Gunther Winkler	Hartwig Steenken
Horses	Faustas	Askan	Torphy	Simone

1972 Germany				
Riders	Hendrik Snoek	K.H. Glebmanus	Lutz Merkel	Alwin Schockemöhle
Horses	Faustas	The Saint	Gonzalas	The Robber
1973 Great Britain				
Riders	Paddy McMahon	Ann Moore	David Broome	Peter Robeson
Horses	Penwood Forge Mills	Psalm	Manhattan	Grebe
1974 Great Britain				
Riders	Harvey Smith	Tony Newbery	David Broome	Peter Robeson
Horses	Salvador III	Warwick III	Sportsman	Grebe
1975 Great Britain				
Riders	Harvey Smith	Paddy McMahon	Graham Fletcher	David Broome
Horses	Salvador III	Penwood Forge Mills	Tuana Dora	Heatwave
1976 Germany				
Riders	Willibert Mehlkopf	Lutz Merkel	Fitz Ligges	Hartwig Steenken
Horses	Faustus	Talvero	Gemnis	Early Warning
1977 Ireland				
Rider	Paul Darragh	James Kernan	Capt. Con Power	Eddie Macken
Horse	Heather Honey	Condy	Coolronan	Boomerang
1978 Ireland				
Riders	Capt. Con Power	James Kernan	Paul Darragh	Eddie Macken
Horses	Castlepark	Condy	Heather Honey	Boomerang
1979 Ireland				
Riders	Paul Darragh	James Kernan	Capt. Con Power	Eddie Macken
Horses	Carroll's Heather Honey	Condy	Rockbarton	Carroll's Boomerang
1980 USA				
Riders	Armand Leone	Katie Monahan	Norman Dello Joio	Melanie Smith

Horses	Wallenstein	Silver Exchange	Allegro	Calypso
1981 Germany				
Riders	Franke Sloothaak	Norbert Koof	Peter Luther	Paul Schockemöhle
Horses	Argonaut	Fire 2	Livius	Deister
1982 Great Britain				
Riders	Harvey Smith	John Whitaker	Malcolm Pyrah	David Broome
Horses	Sanyo Olympic Video	Ryan's Son	Towerlands Chainbridge	Mr Ross
1983 Switzerland				
Riders	Walter Gabathuler	Heidi Robbiani	Willi Melliger	Thomas Fuchs
Horses	Beethoven	Jessica	Van Gogh	Willors Carpets
1984 Ireland				
Riders	Lieut. John Ledingham	George Stewart	Jack Doyle	Eddie Macken
Horses	Gabhran	Leapy Lad	Kerrygold Island	Carroll's El Paso
1985 Great Britain				
Riders	Nick Skelton	Liz Edgar	Robert Smith	John Whitaker
Horses	Everest Apollo	Everest Forever	Olympic Video	Ryan's Son
1986 Great Britain				
Riders	Nick Skelton	Michael Whitaker	Peter Charles	John Whitaker
Horses	Raffles Apollo	Next Warren Point	April Sun	Next Ryan's Son
1987 Ireland				
Riders	Capt. John Ledingham	Jack Doyle	Comdt Gerry Mullins	Eddie Macken
Horses	Gabhran	Hardly	Rockbarton	Carroll's Flight
1988 Great Britain				
Riders	Nick Skelton	Joe Turi	Michael Whitaker	David Broome

Horses	Apollo	Country Classics Kruger	Next Amanda	Queensway Countryman
1989 Great Britain				
Riders	Nick Skelton	David Broome	Joe Turi	John Whitaker
Horses	Burmah Grand Slam	Queensway Lannegan	Country Classics Vital	Next Gammon
1990 Ireland				
Riders	Comdt Gerry Mullins	Edward Doyle	Capt. John Ledingham	Eddie Macken
Horses	Glendalough	Love Me Do	Gabhran	Welfenkrone
1991 Great Britain				
Riders	Nick Skelton	Michael Whitaker	David Broome	John Whitaker
Horses	Alan Paul Phoenix Park	Henderson Gipfelstuermer	Lannegan	Henderson Grannusch
1992 Ireland				
Riders	Peter Charles	Comdt Gerry Mullins	James Kernan	Eddie Macken
Horses	Kruger	Lismore	IJM Touchdown	Welfenkrone
1993 USA				
Riders	Michael Matz	Leslie Lenehan	D.D. Matz	Anne Kursinski
Horses	The General	Gem Twist	Tashiling	Suddenly
1994 Great Britain				
Riders	Nick Skelton	Michael Whitaker	Alison Bradley	John Whitaker
Horses	Everest Limited Edition	Everest Two Step	Endeavour	Everest Grannusch
1995 Ireland				
Riders	Peter Charles	Capt. John Ledingham	Trevor Coyle	Eddie Macken
Horses	La Ina	Kilbaha	Crusing	Miss FAN
1996 Great Britain				
Riders	Nick Skelton	Robert Smith	Di Lampard	John Whitaker

Horses	Dollar Girl	Tees Hanauer	Abbervail Dream	Grannusch

1997 Ireland

Riders	Trevor Coyle	Capt. John Ledingham	Paul Darragh	Eddit Macken
Horses	Cruising	Kilbaha	Scandall XX	FAN Schalkhaar

1998 Italy

Riders	Gianni Govoni	Emanuele Castellini	Alessia Marioni	Guido Dominici
Horses	Loro Piana Las Vegas	Desire	Mardonna Van De Helle	Friso

1999 Netherlands

Riders	Ben Schroder	Carry Huis in't Veld	Leon Thijssen	Jan Tops
Horses	Agrovorm's Athletico	Hay Guy	Garavola	Montemorelos la Silla

2000 Ireland

Riders	Dermott Lennon	Billy Twomey	Jessica Kuerten	Peter Charles
Horses	Liscalgot	Conquest II	Paavo N	Traxdata Amber du Montois

2001 Belgium

Riders	Ludo Philippaerts	Jos Lansink	Marc van Dijck	Stanny van Paesschen
Horses	Parco	AK Caridor Z	Verelst Goliath	O de Pomme

2002 France

Riders	Gilles de Balanda	Christian Hermon	Michel Hecart	Patrice Delaveau
Horses	Crocus Graverie	Ephebe For Ever	Quilano de Kalvarie	Frascator Mail

2003 France

Riders	Florian Angot	Laurent Forrinet	Christian Hermon	Michel Hecart
Horses	First de Launay	Flipper d'Elle	Ephebe For Ever	Quilano de Kalvarie

2004 Ireland				
Riders	Cian O'Connor	Marion Hughes	Jessica Kuerten	Billy Twomey
Horses	Irish Independent Annabella 26	Heritage Fortunas	Quibell	Luidam
2005 Great Britain				
Riders	Nick Skelton	John Whitaker	William Funnell	Michael Whitaker
Horses	Arko III	Exploit du Roulard	Cortaflex Mondriaan	Portofino 63
2006 Germany				
Riders	Thomas Voss	Rene Tebbel	Ulrich Kirchhoff	Heinrich-Hermann Engemann
Horses	Leonardo B	Team Harmony Coupe de Coeur	Carino	Aboyeur W
2007 Germany				
Riders	Thomas Voss	Thomas Muhlbauer	Holger Wulschner	Heinrich-Hermann Engemann
Horses	Leonardo B	Asti Spumante	Clausen	Aboyeur
2008 Great Britain				
Riders	Peter Charles	Tim Gredley	Robert Smith	Nick Skelton
Horses	Murka's Rupert R	Omelli	Vangelis S	Arko III
2009 Italy				
Riders	Juan Carlos Garcia	Giuseppe D'Onofrio	Natale Chiaudani	Piergiorgio Bucci
Horses	Hamilton De Perhet	Landzeu 2	Snai Seldana	Kanebo
2010 Netherlands				
Riders	Eric van der Vleuten	Jur Vrieling	Harrie Smolders	Marc Houtzager
Horses	VDL Groep Utascha	VDL Bubalu	Exquis Walnut de Muze	Tamino

2011 Great Britain				
Riders	Nick Skelton	Michael Whitaker	Scott Brash	Robert Smith
Horses	Carlo 273	Gig Amai	Intertoy Z	Talan
2012 Ireland				
Riders	Clem McMahon	Richie Moloney	Darragh Kerins	Cian O'Connor
Horses	Pacino	Ahorn Van De Zuuthoeve	Lisona	Blue Loyd 12
2013 Great Britain				
Riders	Nick Skelton	Ben Maher	Robert Smith	Scott Brash
Horses	Big Star	Cella	Voila	Hello Sanctos
2014 USA				
Riders	Charlie Jayne	Jessica Springsteen	Katherine A. Dinan	Elizabeth Madden
Horses	Chill R Z	Vindicat W	Nougat du Vallet	Simon
2015 Ireland				
Riders	Bertram Allen	Greg Broderick	Darragh Kenny	Cian O'Connor
Horses	Romanov	MHS Going Global	Sans Souci Z	Good Luck

THE HICKSTEAD DERBY

The Hickstead Derby, as we have seen, produces riders and horses for courses. That angle took a new twist in June 2015, when both the winning horse, Loughnatousa, and rider, Trevor Breen, had won it before, but not together, which made this a first for a horse to win twice with different riders.

Irishman Trevor Breen was also riding the reigning champion, the one-eyed Adventure de Kannan, but he collected eight faults this time.

After winning with the only clear round, Trevor was quick to praise his mount's former rider, Paul Beecher, also from Ireland. He told the Press, 'Paul produced him his whole life so he has to take a lot of the credit – I've only ridden him for a year.'

Date	Horse	Rider	Country
1961	Goodbye	Seamus Hayes	Ireland
1962	Flanagan	Pat Smythe	Great Britain
1963	Gran Geste	Nelson Pessoa	Brazil
1964	Goodbye	Seamus Hayes	Ireland
1965	Gran Geste	Nelson Pessoa	Brazil
1966	Mr Softee	David Broome	Great Britain
1967	Stroller	Marion Coakes	Great Britain
1968	The Maverick VII	Alison Westwood	Great Britain
1969	Xanthos	Anneli Drummond-Hay	Great Britain
1970	Mattie Brown	Harvey Smith	Great Britain
1971	Mattie Brown	Harvey Smith	Great Britain
1972	Shirokko	Hendrik Snoek	Germany
1973	Mr Banbury (The Maverick VII)	Alison Dawes (*née* Westwood)	Great Britain
1974	Salvador	Harvey Smith	Great Britain
1975	Pele	Paul Darragh	Ireland
1976	Boomerang	Eddie Macken	Ireland
1977	Boomerang	Eddie Macken	Ireland
1978	Boomerang	Eddie Macken	Ireland
1979	Boomerang	Eddie Macken	Ireland
1980	Owen Gregory	Michael Whitaker	Great Britain
1981	Sanyo Video	Harvey Smith	Great Britain
1982	Deister	Paul Schockemöhle	Germany
1983	Ryan's Son	John Whitaker	Great Britain
1984	Gabhran	John Ledingham	Ireland
1985	Lorenzo	Paul Schockemöhle	Germany
1986	Deister	Paul Schockemöhle	Germany
1987	J Nick	Nick Skelton	Great Britain
1988	Apollo	Nick Skelton	Great Britain

1989	Apollo	Nick Skelton	Great Britain
1990	Vital	Joe Turi	Great Britain
1991	Mon Santa	Michael Whitaker	Great Britain
1992	Mon Santa	Michael Whitaker	Great Britain
1993	Mon Santa	Michael Whitaker	Great Britain
1994	Kilbaha	John Ledingham	Ireland
1995	Mon Santa	Michael Whitaker	Great Britain
1996	Loro Piana Vivaldi	Nelson Pessoa	Brazil
1997	Bluebird	John Popely	Great Britain
1998	Gammon	John Whitaker	Great Britain
1999	Lionel II	Rob Hoekstra	Great Britain
2000	Virtual Village Welham	John Whitaker	Great Britain
2001	Corrada	Peter Charles	Ireland
2002	Corrada	Peter Charles	Ireland
2003	Corrada	Peter Charles	Ireland
2004	Buddy Bunn	John Whitaker	Great Britain
2005	Alfredo II	Ben Maher	Great Britain
2006	Cortaflex Mondriaan	William Funnell	Great Britain
2007	Cassabachus	Geoff Billington	Great Britain
2008	Cortaflex Mondriaan	William Funnell	Great Britain
2009	Cortaflex Mondriaan	William Funnell	Great Britain
2010	Softrack Skip Two Ramiro	Guy Williams	Great Britain
2011	Promised Land	Tina Fletcher	Great Britain
2012	Loughnatousa WB	Paul Beecher	Ireland
2013	Cartier Z	Philip Miller	Great Britain
2014	Adventure De Kannan	Trevor Breen	Ireland
2015	Loughnatousa WB	Trevor Breen	Ireland

DID YOU KNOW?

The phenomenal pony Stroller, on his favourite jumping ground of Hickstead, won the inaugural Ladies Individual Championship for Marion Mould, *née* Coakes. They won the British Jumping Derby there in 1967 and had clear rounds on two other occasions in a competition in which clear rounds are so rare that it is sometimes won by a horse on four faults.

Having won the Hickstead Derby and being the reigning World Champions, Stroller and Marion were then dropped from the European Championships by the British selectors on the dubious grounds that 'the world champion should not be asked to compete in the European Championships because it is not of the same status'.

Included in the team were Alison Westwood and Anneli Drummond-Hay who, by finishing a creditable fifth and eleventh underlined, in the words of Alan Smith, 'the selectors' woeful decision'.

CLEAR ROUNDS AT HICKSTEAD

1960 Goodbye
1962 Dundrum and Flanagan
1964 Goodbye and Stroller
1966 Mr Softee
1967 Stroller
1968 Stroller and The Maverick (formerly Mr Banbury)
1969 Xanthos
1970 Donald Rex and Mattie Brown
1973 The Maverick
1974 Salvador and Buttevant Boy
1975 Pele and Snaffles
1976 Boomerang
1978 Boomerang

1980 Owen Gregory
1981 Sanyo Video
1983 Ryan's Son
1986 Deister
1987 J Nick
1988 Apollo
1989 Apollo, Viewpoint and Kruger
1990 Apollo and Vital
1991 Mon Santa
1993 Mon Santa, Mr Midnight and Prince D'Incoville
1994 Kilbaha and Partly Cloudy
1995 Kilbaha and Gammon
1998 Kilbaha and Gammon
1999 Lionel II
2000 Lionel II, Traxdata Wiston Bridgit and Virtual Village Welham
2002 Mr Springfield and Corrada
2004 Buddy Bunn and Ak Locarno
2009 Cortaflex Mondriaan
2010 Promised Land and Softrack Skip Two Ramiro
2011 Promised Land
2012 Dorada and Loughnatousa
2013 Cartier Z
2015 Loughnatousa WB

WORLD CHAMPIONSHIPS

Founded in 1978 with the final the following spring, the annual FEI World Cup Show Jumping Competition took hold from the start, with its unique system of the last four riders all competing on their rivals' horses as well as their own in the grand final. This gives a true test of rider ability as well as added interest for the audience.

Today it has all five 'green' continents taking part, divided into fourteen leagues from which the forty-five finalists qualify from some 132 competitions; these are mostly through the winter for the April final. Usually there are twenty riders from Europe, fifteen from America, five from Canada and five from the rest of the world.

The final rotates between countries, and its format ensures a true test, consisting of a table C (speed), followed by a grand prix competition over the first two days and, after one day's rest, a two-round final not against the clock, in which the top four riders swap horses for the final round.

	First	Second	Third
1979 Gothenburg			
Rider	Hugo Simon	Katie Monahan	Eddie Macken and Norman Dello Joio
Horse	Gladstone	The Jones Boy	Carrolls of Dunalk and Allegro
Nation	Austria	USA	Ireland and USA
1980 Baltimore			
Rider	Conrad Homfeld	Melanie Smith	Paul Schockemöhle
Horse	Balbuco	Calypso	El Paso
Nation	USA	USA	Germany
1981 Birmingham			
Rider	Michael Matz	Donald Cheska	Hugo Simon
Horse	Jet Run	Southside	Gladstone
Nation	USA	USA	Austria
1982 Gothenburg			
Rider	Melanie Smith	Paul Schockemöhle	Hugo Simon and John Whitaker
Horse	Calypso	Akrobat	Gladstone and Ryan's Son
Nation	USA	Germany	Austria and Great Britain
1983 Vienna			
Rider	Norman Dello Joio	Hugo Simon	Melanie Smith
Horse	I Love You	Gladstone	Calypso
Nation	USA	Austria	USA
1984 Gothenburg			
Rider	Mario Deslauriers	Norman Dello Joio	Nelson Pessoa
Horse	Aramis	I Love You	Moët & Chandon Larramy
Nation	Canada	USA	Brazil
1985 Berlin			
Rider	Conrad Homfeld	Nick Skelton	Pierre Durand
Horse	Abdullah	Everest St James	Jappeloup

Nation	USA	Great Britain	France
1986 Gothenburg			
Rider	Leslie Burr Lenehan	Ian Millar	Conrad Homfeld
Horse	McLain	Big Ben	Maybe
Nation	USA	Canada	USA
1987 Paris			
Rider	Katherine Burdsall	Philippe Rozier	Lisa Jacquin
Horse	The Natural	Malesan Jiva	For the Moment
Nation	USA	France	USA
1988 Gothenburg			
Rider	Ian Millar	Pierre Durand	Philippe Le Jeune
Horse	Big Ben	Jappeloup de Luze	Nistria
Nation	Canada	France	Belgium
1989 Tampa			
Rider	Ian Millar	John Whitaker	George Lindeman
Horse	Big Ben	Next Milton	Jupiter
Nation	Canada	Great Britain	USA
1990 Dortmund			
Rider	John Whitaker	Pierre Durand	Franke Sloothaak
Horse	Henderson Milton	Jappeloup	Walzerkönig
Nation	Great Britain	France	Germany
1991 Gothenburg			
Rider	John Whitaker	Nelson Pessoa	Roger-Yves Bost
Horse	Henderson Milton	Special Envoy	Norton de Rhuys
Nation	Great Britain	Brazil	France
1992 Del Mar			
Rider	Thomas Frügmann	Lesley McNaught-Mändli	Markus Fuchs
Horse	Bockmann's Genius	Moët & Chandon Pirol	Interpane Shandor
Nation	Austria	Switzerland	Switzerland
1993 Gothenburg			
Rider	Ludger Beerbaum	John Whitaker	Michael Matz

Horse	Almox Ratina	Everest Grannusch & Everest Milton	Rhum
Nation	Germany	Great Britain	USA
1994 'S-Hertogenbosch			
Rider	Jos Lansink	Franke Sloothaak	Michael Whitaker
Horse	Bollvorms Libero H	Dorina & Weihaiwej	Midnight Madness
Nation	Netherlands	Germany	Great Britain
1995 Gothenburg			
Rider	Nick Skelton	Lars Nieberg	Lesley McNaught-Mändli
Horse	Everest Dollar Girl	For Pleasure	Barcelona SVH & Doenhoff
Nation	Great Britain	Germany	Switzerland
1996 Geneve			
Rider	Hugo Simon	Willi Melliger	Nick Skelton
Horse	E.T.	Calvaro V	Dollar Girl
Nation	Austria	Switzerland	Great Britain
1997 Gothenburg			
Rider	Hugo Simon	John Whitaker	Franke Sloothaak
Horse	E.T.	Grannush & Welham	San Patrignano Joly
Nation	Austria	Great Britain	Germany
1998 Helsinki			
Rider	Rodrigo Pessoa	Lars Nieberg	Ludger Beerbaum
Horse	Loro Piana & Baloubet de Rouet	Esprit	P.S. Priamos
Nation	Brazil	Germany	Germany
1999 Gothenburg			
Rider	Rodrigo Pessoa	Trevor Coyle	René Tebbel
Horse	Grandini Baloubet du Rouet	Cruising	Radiator
Nation	Brazil	Ireland	Germany
2000 Las Vegas			
Rider	Rodrigo Pessoa	Markus Fuchs	Beat Mändli

Horse	Baloubet du Rouet	Tinkas Boy	Pozitano
Nation	Brazil	Switzerland	Switzerland
2001 Gothenburg			
Rider	Markus Fuchs	Rodrigo Pessoa	Michael Whitaker
Horse	Tinka's Boy	Baloubet du Rouet	Handel II
Nation	Switzerland	Brazil	Great Britain
2002 Leipzig			
Rider	Otto Becker	Ludger Beerbaum	Rodrigo Pessoa
Horse	Dobels Cento	Gladdys S	Baloubet du Rouet
Nation	Germany	Germany	Brazil
2003 Las Vegas			
Rider	Marcus Ehning	Rodrigo Pessoa	Malin Baryard
Horse	Anka	Baloubet du Rouet	H&M Butterfly Flip
Nation	Germany	Brazil	Sweden
2004 Milan			
Rider	Bruno Broucqsault	Meredith Michaels-Beerbaum	Markus Fuchs
Horse	Dileme de Cephe	Shutterfly	Tinka's Boy
Nation	France	Germany	Switzerland
2005 Las Vegas			
Rider	Meredith Michaels-Beerbaum	Michael Whitaker	Marcus Ehning and Lars Nieberg
Horse	Shutterfly	Portofino	Gitania and Lucie
Nation	Germany	Great Britain	Germany and Germany
2006 Kuala Lumpur			
Rider	Marcus Ehning	Jessica Kürten	Beat Mändli
Horse	Sandro Boy	Castle Forbes Libertina	Ideo du Thot
Nation	Germany	Ireland	Switzerland
2007 Las Vegas			
Rider	Beat Mändli	Daniel Deusser	Markus Beerbaum and Steve Guerdat

Horse	Ideo du Thot	Air Jordan Z	Leena and Tresir
Nation	Switzerland	Germany	Germany and Switzerland

2008 Gothenburg			
Rider	Meredith Michaels-Beerbaum	Rich Fellers	Heinrich-Herman Engemann
Horse	Shutterfly	Flexible	Aboyeur
Nation	Germany	USA	Germany

2009 Las Vegas			
Rider	Meredith Michael-Beerbaum	McLain Ward	Albert Zoer
Horse	Shutterfly	Sapphire	Okidoki
Nation	Germany	USA	Netherlands

2010 Le Grand-Saconnex			
Rider	Marcus Ehning	Ludger Beerbaum and Pius Schwizer	-
Horse	Noltes Küchengirl & Plot Blue	Gotha and Ulysse & Carlina	-
Nation	Germany	Germany and Switzerland	-

2011 Leipzig			
Rider	Christian Ahlmann	Eric Lamaze	Jeroen Dubbeldam
Horse	Taloubet Z	Hickstead	Simon
Nation	Germany	Canada	Austria

2012 'S-Hertogenbosch			
Rider	Rich Fellers	Steve Guerdat	Pius Schwizer
Horse	Flexible	Nino des Buissonnets	Ulysse & Carlina
Nation	USA	Switzerland	Switzerland

2013 Gothenburg			
Rider	Beezie Madden	Steve Guerdat	Kevin Staut
Horse	Simon	Nino des Buissonnets	Silvana
Nation	USA	Switzerland	France

2014 Lyon			
Rider	Daniel Deusser	Ludger Beerbaum	Scott Brash
Horse	Cornet d'Armour	Chaman & Chiara 222	Ursula XII
Nation	Germany	Germany	Great Britain
2015 Las Vegas			
Rider	Steve Gyerdat	Pénélope Leprevost	Bertram Allen
Horse	Albfuehren's Paille	Vagabond de la Pomme	Molly Malone V
Nation	Switzerland	France	Ireland

EUROPEAN CHAMPIONSHIPS

Begun in 1957, the European Championships are 22 years older than the World Cup, and are held every two years, in the gap years between the Olympic Games and World Equestrian Games. To begin with, until 1973, only the Olympic year was missed. Team championships were introduced in 1975; before that the title only went to individual riders.

Among the early British individual winners were David Broome three times, David Barker in the 1960s, Paddy MacMahon in 1973 and John Whitaker in 1989 (the last Briton to do so).

Featuring among the British silver- and bronze-medal winners over the years were Harvey Smith, John and Michael Whitaker (both of them several times), Malcolm Pyrah and Nick Skelton.

In 2013, two of the British Olympic gold-medal team, Ben Maher and Scott Brash, were joined by William Funnell and Michael Whitaker to add the team European gold medal to their tally. Ben Maher, and Scott Brash riding his Olympic horse Hello Sanctos, also took the individual silver and bronze medals behind Frenchman Roger Yvres Bost.

The 2015 Individual title saw a nail-biting final in which Ireland's Bertram Allen finished a close third at only 19 years of age.

The European Championships also take place for young riders, juniors, ponies, children and veterans.

Individual Results

	First	Second	Third
1957 Rotterdam			
Rider	Hans Günter Winkler	Bernard Oppes Fombelle	Salvatore

Horse	Sonnenglanz Halla	Bucephale	Pagoro 24
Nation	West Germany	France	Italy
1958 Aachen			
Rider	Fritz Thiedemann	Piero D'Inzeo	Hans Günter Winkler
Horse	Meteor	The Rock	Halla
Nation	West Germany	Italy	Germany
1959 Paris			
Rider	Piero D'Inzeo	Pierre J. d'Oriola	Fritz Thiedemann
Horse	Uruguay	Virtuoso	Godewind
Nation	Italy	France	West Germany
1960 No competition			
1961 Aachen			
Rider	David Broome	Piero D'Inzeo	Hans Günter Winkler
Horse	Sunsalve	The Rock	Feuerdorn Romanus
Nation	Great Britain	Italy	West Germany
1962 London			
Rider	David Barker	Hans Günter Winkler	Piero D'Inzeo
Horse	Mr Softee	Feuerdorn Romanus	The Rock
Nation	Great Britain	West Germany	Italy
1963 Rome			
Rider	Graziano Mancinelli	Alwin Schockemöhle	Harvey Smith
Horse	Rockette	Freiherr	O'Malley
Nation	Italy	West Germany	Great Britain
1964 No competition			
1965 Aachen			
Rider	Hermann Schridde	Nelson Pessoa	Alwin Schockemöhle
Horse	Kamerad	Huipil	Axakt
Nation	West Germany	Brazil	West Germany

1966 Lucerne			
Rider	Nelson Pessoa	Frank Chapot	Hugo Miguel Arrambide
Horse	Huipil	Good Twist	Chimbote
Nation	Brazil	USA	Argentina
1967 Rotterdam			
Rider	David Broome	Harvey Smith	Alwin Schockemöhle
Horse	Mr Softee	Harvester	Pesgö
Nation	Great Britain	Great Britain	West Germany
Competition becomes biennial			
1969 Hickstead			
Rider	David Broome	Alwin Schockemöhle	Hans Günter Winkler
Horse	Mr Softee	Donald Rex	Enigk
Nation	Great Britain	West Germany	West Germany
1971 Aachen			
Rider	Hartwig Steenken	Harvey Smith	Paul Weier
Horse	Simona	Evan Jones	Wulf
Nation	West Germany	Great Britain	Switzerland
1973 Hickstead			
Rider	Paddy McMahon	Alwin Schockemöhle	Hubert Parot
Horse	Penwood Forge Mill	The Robber	Tic
Nation	Great Britain	West Germany	France
1975 Munich			
Rider	Alwin Schockemöhle	Hartwig Steenken	Sönke Sönksen
Horse	Warwick	Erle	Kwept
Nation	West Germany	West Germany	West Germany
1977 Vienna			
Rider	Johan Heins	Eddie Macken	Toon Ebben
Horse	Seven Valleys	Kerrygold	Jumbo Design
Nation	Netherlands	Ireland	Netherlands

1979 Rotterdam			
Rider	Gerd Wiltfang	Paul Schockemöhle	Hugo Simon
Horse	Roman	Deister	Gladstone
Nation	West Germany	West Germany	Austria
1981 Munich			
Rider	Paul Schockemöhle	Malcolm Pyrah	Bruno Candrian
Horse	Deister	Anglezarke	Van Gogh
Nation	West Germany	Great Britain	Switzerland
1983 Hickstead			
Rider	Paul Schockemöhle	John Whitaker	Frédéric Cottier
Horse	Deister	Ryan's Son	Flambeau
Nation	West Germany	Great Britain	France
1985 Dinard			
Rider	Paul Schockemöhle	Heidi Robbiani	John Whitaker
Horse	Deister	Jessica	Hopscotch
Nation	West Germany	Switzerland	Great Britain
1987 St Gallen			
Rider	Pierre Durand	John Whitaker	Nick Skelton
Horse	Jappeloup	Milton	Apollo
Nation	France	Great Britain	Great Britain
1989 Rotterdam			
Rider	John Whitaker	Michael Whitaker	Jos Lansink
Horse	Milton	Mon Santa	Felix
Nation	Great Britain	Great Britain	Netherlands
1991 La Baule			
Rider	Eric Navet	Franke Sloothaak	Jos Lansink
Horse	Quito de Baussy	Walzerkönig	Egano
Nation	France	Germany	Netherlands
1993 Gijon			
Rider	Willi Melliger	Michael Robert	Michael Whitaker

Horse	Quinta	Miss S.P.	Midnight Madness
Nation	Switzerland	France	Great Britain

1995 St Gillen

Rider	Peter Charles	Michael Whitaker	Willi Melliger
Horse	La Ina	Ev. Two Step	Calvaro V
Nation	Ireland	Great Britain	Switzerland

1997 Mannheim

Rider	Ludger Beerbaum	Hugo Simon	Willi Melliger
Horse	Ratina	E.T. FRH	Calvaro V
Nation	Germany	Austria	Switzerland

1999 Hickstead

Rider	Alexandra Ledermann	Markus Fuchs	Lesley Mc Naught
Horse	Rochet M	Tinkas Boy	Dulf
Nation	France	Switzerland	Switzerland

2001 Arnhem

Rider	Ludger Beerbaum	Ludo Philippaerts	Rolf-Göran Bengtsson
Horse	Gladdys	Verelst Otterongo	Isovlas Pialotta
Nation	Germany	Belgium	Sweden

2003 Donaueschingen

Rider	Christian Ahlmann	Ludger Beerbaum	Marcus Ehning
Horse	Coester	Goldfever	For Pleasure
Nation	Germany	Germany	Germany

2005 San Patrignano

Rider	Marco Kutscher	Christina Liebherr	Jeroen Dubbeldam
Horse	Montender	L.B. No Mercy	BMC Nassau
Nation	Germany	Switzerland	Netherlands

2007 Mannheim

Rider	Meredith Michaels-Beerbaum	Jos Lansink	Ludger Beerbaum
Horse	Shutterfly	Al-Kaheel Cavalor Cumano	Goldfesver
Nation	Germany	Netherlands	Germany

2009 Windsor			
Rider	Kevin Staut	Carsten-Otto Nagel	Albert Zoer
Horse	Kraque Boom	Corradina	Okidoki
Nation	France	Germany	Netherlands
2011 Madrid			
Rider	Rolf-Göran Bengtsson	Carsten-Otto Nagel	Nick Skelton
Horse	Ninja la Silla	Corradina	Carlo
Nation	Sweden	Germany	Great Britain
2013 Herning			
Rider	Roger Yves Bost	Ben Baher	Scott Brash
Horse	Castle Forbes Myrtille Paulois	Cella	Hello Sanctos
Nation	France	Great Britain	Great Britain

Team Results

	First	Second	Third
1975 Munich			
Riders	Alwin Schockemöhle, Hartwig Steenken, Sönke Sönksen, Hendrik Snoek	Paul Weier, Walter Gabathuler, Bruno Candrian, Jurg Friedli	Marcel Rozier, Gilles Bertrand de Balanda, Michel Roche, Hubert Parot
Horses	Warwick, Erle, Kwept, Rasputin	Wulf, Butterfly, Golden Shuttle, Firebird	Bayard de Maupas, Bearn, Un Espoir, Rivage
Nation	West Germany	Switzerland	France
1977 Vienna			
Riders	Harry Wouters van der Oudenweyer, Anton Ebben, Henk Nooren, Johan Heins	Derek Ricketts, Debbie Johnsey, Harvey Smith, David Broome	Norbert Koof, Lutz Merkel, Paul Schockemöhle, Gerd Wiltfang

Horses	Salerno, Jumbo Design, Pluco, Seven Valleys	Hydrophane Coldsteam, Moxy, Olympic Star, Philco	Minister, Salvaro, Agent, Davos
Nation	Netherlands	Great Britain	West Germany

1979 Rotterdam

Riders	Malcolm Pyrah, Derek Ricketts, Caroline Bradley, David Broome	Heinrich Wilhelm Johannsmann, Peter Luther, Paul Schockemöhle, Gerd Wiltfang	John Roche, Gerry Mullins, Con Power, Eddie Macken
Horses	Law Court, Hydrophane Coldstream, Tigre, Queensway Big Q	Sarto, Livius, Deister, Roman	Maigh Cuillin, Ballinderry, Rockbarton, Carroll's Boomerang
Nation	Great Britain	West Germany	Ireland

1981 Munich

Rider	Norbert Koof, Peter Luther, Gerd Wiltfang, Paul Schockemöhle	Willi Melliger, Walter Gabathuler, Thomas Fuchs, Bruno Candrian	Emile Hendrix, Rob Ehrens, Henk Nooren, Johan Heins
Horse	Fire, Livius, Roman, Deister	Trumpf Buur, Harley, Willora Carpets, Van Gogh	Livius, Koh-I-Noor, Opstalan II, Larramy
Nation	West Germany	Switzerland	Netherlands

1983 Hickstead

Rider	Walter Gabathuler, Heidi Robbiani, Willi Melliger, Thomas Fuchs	Harvey Smith, David Broome, John Whitaker, Malcolm Pyrah	Achaz von Buchwaldt, Michael Rüping, Gerd Wiltfang, Paul Schockemöhle
Horse	Beethoven II, Jessica V, Van Gogh, Willora Swiss	Sanyo Olympic Video, Mr Ross, Ryan's Son, Towerlands Anglezarke	Wendy, Caletto, Goldika, Deister
Nation	Switzerland	Great Britain	West Germany

1985 Dinard

Rider	Nick Skelton, Michael Whitaker, Malcolm Pyrah, John Whitaker	Philippe Guerdat, Heidi Robbiani, Walter Gabathuler, Willi Melliger	Franke Sloothaak, Michael Rüping, Peter Luther, Paul Schockemöhle

Horse	Everest St James, Warren Point, Towerlands Anglezarke, Hopscotch	Pybalia, Jessica V, The Swan, Beethoven II	Walido, Silbersee, Livius, Deister
Nation	Great Britain	Switzerland	West Germany

1987 St Gallen

Rider	Nick Skelton, Michael Whitaker, Malcolm Pyrah, John Whitaker	Philippe Rozier, Pierre Durand, Frédéric Cottier, Michel Robert	Philippe Guerdat, Markus Fuchs, Walter Gabathuler, Willi Melliger
Horse	Raffles Apollo, Next Amanda, Towerlands Anglezarke, Next Milton	Jiva Malesan, Jappeloup de Luze, Flambeau, Pequignet Lafayette	Lanciano V, Shandor II, The Swan, Malesan Bordeau Corso
Nation	Great Britain	France	Switzerland

1989 Rotterdam

Rider	Nick Skelton, Michael Whitaker, Joe Turi, John Whitaker	Hervé Godignon, Philippe Rozier, Michel Robert, Pierre Durand	Walter Gabathuler, Markus Fuchs, Willi Melliger, Thomas Fuchs
Horse	Burmah Apollo, Next Monsanta, Country Classics Kruger, Next Milton	Moët & Chandon La Belletière, Oscar Minotière Malésan, Pequignet Lafayette, Jappeloup de Luze	Moët & Chandon The Swan, Moët & Chandon Shandor, Moët & Chandon Corso, Moët & Chandon Dollar Girl
Nation	Great Britain	France	Switzerland

1991 La Baule

Rider	Piet Raijmakers, Jan Tops, Emile Hendrix, Jos Lansink	Nick Skelton, Michael Whitaker, David Broome, John Whitaker	Willi Melliger, Markus Fuchs, Rudolf Letter, Thomas Fuchs
Horse	Ratina Z, Top Gun La Silla, Optiebeurs Aldato, Optiebeurs Egano	Phoenix Park, Henderson Mon Santa, Lannegan, Henderson Milton	Quinta, Shandor, Nascon Cartier, Dollar Girl
Nation	Netherlands	Great Britain	Switzerland

1993 Gijon			
Rider	Willi Melliger, Lesley McNaught-Mändli, Stefan Lauber, Thomas Fuchs	Nick Skelton, Michael Whitaker, Mark Armstrong, John Whitaker	Hubert Bourdy, Michel Robert, Hervé Godignon, Eric Navet
Horse	Quinta C, Pirol IV, Lugana II, Dylano	Everest Dollar Girl, Everest Midnight Madness, Corella, Everest Gammon	San Patrignano Razzia, Miss San Patrignano, Twist du Valon, Waiti Quito de Baussy
Nation	Switzerland	Great Britain	France
1995 St Gillen			
Rider	Willi Melliger, Lesley McNaught, Stefan Lauber, Thomas Fuchs	Nick Skelton, Michael Whitaker, Alison Bradley, John Whitaker	Hervé Godignon, Jean-Maurice Bonneau, Alexandra Ledermann, Roger-Yves Bost
Horse	Calvaro, Doenhoff, Baby Network Escado, Major AC Folien	Everest Dollar Girl, Everest Two Step, Endeavour, Everest Welham	Unic du Perchis, Pironniere, Rochet, Souviens Toi III
Nation	Switzerland	Great Britain	France
1997 Mannheim			
Rider	Lars Nieberg, Markus Beerbaum, Ludger Beerbaum, Markus Merschformann	Emile Hendrix, Bert Romp, Jan Tops, Jos Lansink	Michael Whitaker, Geoff Billington, Robert Smith, John Whitaker
Horse	For Pleasure, Lady Weingard, Sprehe Ratina Z, Ballerina	Ten Cate Finesse, Burg's Mr Blue, Top Gun Las Silla, Nissan Calvaro Z	Virtual Village Ashley, Virtual Village It's Otto, Senator Tees Hanauer, Virtual Village Welham
Nation	Germany	Netherlands	Great Britain
1999 Hickstead			
Rider	Carsten-Otto Nagel, Meredith Michaels-Beerbaum, Marcus Ehning, Ludger Beerbaum	Lesley McNaught, Markus Fuchs, Beat Mändli, Willi Melliger	Emile Hendrix, Jeroen Dubbeldam, Jan Tops, Jos Lansink

Horse	L'Eperon, Sprehe Stella, For Pleasure, Champion du Lys	Dulf, Tinka's Boy, Pozitano, Calvaro	RBG Finesse, V&L De Sjiem, Montemorelos La Silla, Nissan Carthago Z
Nation	Germany	Switzerland	Netherlands

2001 Arnhem

Rider	Kevin Babington, Jessica Kürten, Peter Charles, Dermott Lennon	Malin Baryard, Helena Lundbäck, Rolf-Göran Bengtsson, Peter Eriksson	Sören von Rönne, Otto Becker, Lars Nieberg, Ludger Beerbaum
Horse	Carling King, Bonita, Traxdata Corrado, Liscalgot	H&M Butterfly Flip, Utfors Mynta, Isovlas Pialotta, VDL Cardento	Chandra, Dobel's Cento, Esprit FRH, Gladdys S
Nation	Ireland	Sweden	Germany

2003 Donaueschingen

Rider	Marcus Ehning, Christian Ahlmann, Ludger Beerbaum, Otto Becker	Michel Robert, Eric Levallois, Michel Hécart, Reynald Angot	Beat Mändli, Steve Guerdat, Markus Fuchs, Willi Melliger
Horse	For Pleasure, Cöster, Goldfever, Dobel's Cento	Galet d'Auzay, Diamant de Semilly, Quilano de Kalvarie, Tlaloc M	Pozitano, Tepic La Silla, Tinka's Boy, Gold du Talus
Nation	Germany	France	Switzerland

2005 San Patrignano

Rider	Marcus Ehning, Christian Ahlmann, Marco Kutscher, Meredith Michaels-Beerbaum	Fabio Crotta, Steve Guerdat, Christina Liebherr, Markus Fuchs	Gerco Schröder, Leon Thijssen, Jeroen Dubbeldam, Yves Houtackers
Horse	Gitania, Cöster, Montender, Checkmate	Madame Pompadour M, Isovlas Pialotta, LB No Mercy, La Toya III	Eurocommerce Monaco, Nairobi, BMC Nassau, Gran Corrado
Nation	Germany	Switzerland	Netherlands

2007 Mannheim			
Rider	Vincent Voorn, Jeroen Dubbeldam, Albert Zoer, Gerco Schröder	Marcus Ehning, Christian Ahlmann, Meredith Michaels-Beerbaum, Ludger Beerbaum	Michael Whitaker, David McPherson, Ellen Whitaker, John Whitaker
Horse	Audi's Alpapillon-Armanie, BMC Up and Down, Okidoki, Eurocommerce Berlin	Noltes Küchengirl, Cöster, Shutterfly, Goldfever	Suncal Portofino, Pilgrim II, Locarno, Peppermill
Nation	Netherlands	Germany	Great Britain
2009 Windsor			
Rider	Pius Schwizer, Daniel Etter, Steve Guerdat, Clarissa Crotta	Juan-Carlos Garcia, Giuseppi d'Onofrio, Natale Chiaudani, Piergiorgio Bucci	Marcus Ehning, Carsten-Otto Nagel, Thomas Mühlbauer, Meredith Michaels-Beerbaum
Horse	Ulysse, Peu à Peu, Jalisca Solier, West Side v °Meerputhoeve	Hamilton de Perhet, Landzeu, Snai Seldana di Campalto, Kanebo	Plot Blue, Corradina, Asti Spumante, Checkmate
Nation	Switzerland	Italy	Germany
2011 Madrid			
Rider	Marco Kutscher, Carsten-Otto Nagel, Janne Friederike Meyer, Ludger Beerbaum	Michel Robert, Pénélope Leprevost, Kevin Staut, Olivier Guillon	Nick Skelton, Guy Williams, Ben Maher, John Whitaker
Horse	Cornet Obolensky, Corradina, Lambrasco, Gotha FRH	Kellemoi de Pepita, Mylord Carthago, Silvana, Lord de Theize	Carlo, Titus, Tripple X III, Peppermill
Nation	Germany	France	Great Britain
2013 Herning			
Rider	Ben Maher, Michael Whitaker, William Funnell, Scott Brash	Daniel Deusser, Carsten-Otto Nagel, Christian Ahlmann, Ludger Beerbaum	Jens Fredricson, Angelica Augustsson, Henrik von Eckermann, Rolf-Göran Bengtsson

Horse	Cella, Viking, Billy Congo, Hello Sanctos	Cornet d'Amour, Corradina, Codex One, Chiara	Lunatic, Mic Mac du Tillard, Gotha FRH, Casall Ask
Nation	Great Britain	Germany	Sweden

HORSE HUMOUR

Heavenly Horse Show

One day in heaven, Saint Peter, Saint Paul and Saint John were standing around near the horse paddocks watching the horses frolic.

'I am certainly bored,' stated John.

'Me too,' Paul chimed in.

Peter stood and watched the horses. 'I know!' Peter began. 'Why don't we have a horse show?'

Paul and John thought that the idea was great except for one small detail that Paul pointed out.

'Who are we to compete against, Peter?' Paul asked.

The trio pondered a moment when Peter realised the answer. 'We will call up Satan and invite him to the horse show. I mean, we have all of the finest horses here in heaven, all of the World and National Champions are here. His stable is ridden with the spoiled, difficult and mean horses. We are certain to win at the show!'

And so the trio called up Satan on the other realm communication lines and invited him to their horse show. Satan laughed and asked why they would want to be humiliated like that, because he would certainly beat them.

Peter, Paul and John did not understand. 'What do you mean, Satan?' Peter asked. 'We have all of the National and World Champion horses in our stable in heaven. How could you possibly beat us?'

Satan paused a moment and then laughed. 'Have you forgotten so soon, gentlemen? I have all the judges!'

BIBLIOGRAPHY

Judith Draper, *The Stars of Show Jumping* (Stanley Paul, 1990)

Judith Draper, *Show Jumping, Records, Facts and Champions* (Guinness Books, 1987)

Anne Holland, *Drugs and Horses* (Compass Equestrian, 2000)

Anne Holland, *Ireland's Mr Show Jumping* (The Liffey Press, 2014)

Pamela Macgregor-Morris, *The World's Show Jumpers* (Macdonald, 1955)

Ann Martin, *The Edgars Forever* (Pelham Books, 1984)